Blurring the Edges

Integrated Curriculum Through Writing and Children's Literature

Barbara Chatton
and
N. Lynne Decker Collins

HEINEMANN

Portsmouth, NH

Heinemann
A division of Reed Elsevier Inc.
361 Hanover Street
Portsmouth, NH 03801-3912
http://www.heinemann.com

Offices and agents throughout the world

The author and publisher thank those who generously gave permission to reprint borrowed material.

Portions of the book first appeared in "Blurring the Edges: Integrated Curriculum Through Writing and Children's Literature: Always Wondering" by Barbara Chatton and Norma Decker Collins. *Writing Teacher*, Vol. 8, No. 5, May 1995, pp. 18–21; and "Integrating Reading and Writing Instruction: Blurring the Edges" by Barbara Chatton and Norma Decker Collins. *Writing Teacher*, Vol. 6, No.3, January 1993, pp.28–33.

Library of Congress Cataloging-in-Publication Data
Chatton, Barbara.
    Blurring the edges: integrated curriculum through writing and children's literature /
Barbara Chatton and N. Lynne Decker Collins.
       p.   cm.
    Includes bibliographical references (p.   ) and index.
    ISBN 0-325-00144-8 (alk. paper)
    1. Language arts—Correlation with content subjects.
  2. Children's literature—Study and teaching (Elementary)
  3. Interdisciplinary approach in education.   4. Children—Books and reading.
  I. Collins, N. Lynne Decker. II. Title.
LB1576.C46   1999   98-50477
372.6'043—dc21   CIP

Editor: William Varner
Production: Melissa L. Inglis
Cover design: Darci Mehall
Manufacturing: Louise Richardson

Printed in the United States of America on acid-free paper
03 02 01 00 99 RRD 1 2 3 4 5

We dedicate this book to our mothers who
were both readers, writers, and fine cooks.

Mildred Vick Chatton
1916–1994

Merry Estelle Caillier
1928–1990

Contents

Acknowledgments

One of the most important aspects of our work as teachers is the sense of collaboration that comes from sharing experiences of reading and writing. We want to acknowledge the supportive community of friends and colleagues who have encouraged us as we have worked on this book. When we began to develop our concept of blurring the edges, Mike O' Laughlin was a key voice in our conversations. Work from his dissertation comparing the writing processes of children's authors with the processes of characters in their works is used here with gratitude. He has also served as our editorial assistant, checking references, organizing resources, and providing good-natured help when it was most needed.

Anyone who works with children's literature knows that our job is made easier and more pleasurable because of the help we receive and the conversations about books we have with librarians and booksellers. We want to thank Anita Trout, at the Albany County Library; Laurn Wilhelm, at the Learning Resources Center at the University of Wyoming; Amy Shaw, from The Second Story Bookstore; and Linda Goldman, from Chickering Bookstore in Laramie, for their advice and suggestions. Numerous teachers in the Wyoming schools and at the University have been our inspiration and our best collaborators as we've grown in the process of teaching and learning.

Amy Cohn, who suggested we try to write this manuscript, and Bill Varner who carried us through, have earned our gratitude for their constructive suggestions and professionalism. The Division of Lifelong Learning and Instruction at the University of Wyoming provided financial support for the manuscript development.

We want to especially thank Andy Bryson and Jim Collins, our spouses, for software assistance, helpful chores, and remaining calm during the frantic moments of passing manuscripts back and forth.

to factual writing, from journal entries to essays. The strict lines among disciplines are transcended in the world around us. Individuals do not express themselves in only one way. Scientists can also be poets. Writers of fiction can be historians. Artists can be authors.

Before going further with our blurring metaphor, we attempted to define it. We probed our beliefs, practices, and professional lives for insights and understanding. We knew we practiced "blurring the edges" in our workshops with teachers, and we knew we did it in our own classrooms. Even though a clear-cut definition was difficult to discern, three philosophical themes contributed to our notion of what the metaphor means.

First, we were comfortable with early childhood programs and classrooms in which developmentally appropriate practice and play-based curricula were used successfully to help children make sense of the world around them. Most of us have observed the playfulness of young children. Like the authors in Bergen's *Play as a Medium for Learning and Development* (1987), we understood that, for children, play can be serious work for powerful learning. Young children quite naturally experiment with objects, act out roles, practice their language with others, and create rules as they try out what they have learned from books, parents, and television. This play can involve repetitions of writing and drawings until something is right, self-correcting of language miscues, and lots of questioning of the reasons things work as they do. We believe that this playful attitude toward learning—one that is experimental, intrinsically motivated, and constructive—can work well with all elementary school children, although tasks become more sophisticated.

Second, we were aware that postmodern criticism suggests that we have arbitrarily created disciplines within literature to help us order the world of reading and writing. In a time of paradigm changes, authors no longer hold to particular narrow topics and forms, but move easily across genres to express their ideas. Anyone who has ever tried to help students make decisions about the differences among short stories, novellas, and novels has experienced this difficulty. Avi's *Nothing but the Truth* is a novel made up entirely of documents and letters. Karen Hesse's Newbery award–winning *Out of the Dust* is written as a series of poems.

Authors, illustrators, and filmmakers sometimes use *pastiche*, a technique in which styles, themes, and allusions are borrowed and pasted together to create new meanings, forcing us to rethink what we already know. Author–illustrator Chris Van Allsburg, for example, provides a new twist on Dr. Seuss' *The Cat in the Hat* in his picture book, *Jumanji*, a story that also considers the consequences of letting an outside influence into the house when your parents aren't home, having a wild time, then managing to return to normal before they return. In another picture book, Van Allsburg takes the seven wonders of the world and drowns them in *Ben's Dream*. David Macaulay takes apart the Empire State Building in *Unbuilding*. Author Berkeley Breathed tells a fantasy story of a much longed for bicycle in *Red Ranger Came Calling*, then provides a photograph of a bicycle embedded in a tree at the end of the book to show the reality of the story. These authors are producing works that do not fit neatly into traditional literary genres. We spend a great deal of time trying to help students identify genres, but when presented with these modern works, our old definitions don't fit.

Third, we wanted to take interdisciplinary events into account. Steven Tchudi and Stephen Lafer suggested that *interdisciplinary* was a broad term used whenever teachers help students to see a relationship between or among traditional disciplines (Tchudi & Lafer 1996). They pointed out that these disciplines were developed over time by scholars to help organize and manage growing bodies of knowledge and the ways of thinking about them. But the hard and fast lines among disciplines are breaking down even at the highest levels of scholarship. Much modern study is interdisciplinary. Scientists, for example, must study global systems, interactions of people, and history to make sense of environmental problems. Anthropologists must consider story, politics, and art to make sense of a culture. Physicists attempt to explain the abstract notions of the universe through poetic language and analogy, as well as through mathematical equations. Writings that explore these problems from a variety of perspectives are increasingly common in the literature for both adults and children.

Some historians are now engaging in speculative history, in which they try to imagine what would have occurred in the past if a single event had not taken place, if a leader had not died, if a shot had not been fired, or if the victor had not won. This "What if?" approach to history sounds more like historical fiction than history. Yet, these historians build the case that we learn about the randomness of events and the power of human nature from the past and that in probing the past we can better understand the present. In fact, many teachers have successfully integrated historical fiction into their social studies curriculum to help their students understand the personalities and decisions of the people involved in historic acts.

The world in which we live is one of blurred distinctions. We read the recipe for our favorite cookies, use math to measure ingredients, watch chemistry occur as baking soda mixes with other elements, and enjoy the sensory experience of eating warm cookies straight from the oven. Without thinking, we perform the tasks of a mathematician, a scientist, and an artist. It is this kind of blurring that is encouraged and discussed in the following chapters.

From our teaching experiences, we know that moving among disciplines requires a certain kind of learning environment, one that includes diverse opportunities for students to read and write, to think and wonder, and to speculate and examine. Such environments are permeable and allow for fluid movements across disciplines. Students and teachers are neither locked into fixed ideas about how to organize the day or the curriculum nor limited in their choice of ways to represent what they know. Instead, each new idea or discovery, each book read and enjoyed, each poem or story listened to expands their understanding and allows students to reflect, rethink, and reorganize their views of the world. Because such opportunities are available in social studies, science, and mathematics as well as in language arts, we want to focus on the linkages that exist among them. We want to look for writing and reading in places that we don't usually look.

Our ideas are shaped not only from theories about early childhood education, postmodern criticism, and interdisciplinary study, but also from teaching and learning theories. Based on our belief that children bring diverse background experiences to classrooms, that learning must be adjusted to accommodate the differences, and that learning and language are related, we imagine an elementary curriculum that is expansive rather than restrictive. The curriculum we describe in the following chapters embraces multidimensional teaching and learning. It searches out reading and writing in ordinary places, celebrating the processes of learning as well as its products.

Throughout this book, students are invited to "see" through several lenses. We want students to snoop around and play around in a variety of languages, including the language of mathematicians, scientists, historians, and others. We want scientists to see what poets see, and to feel comfortable expressing their findings poetically; we want historians to see what mathematicians see, and to discuss their insights mathematically. We want journalists to see the way artists see, and to represent their investigations visually. We want to blur the language of reading and writing instruction with the language of other disciplines.

In this sense, we embrace a collage curriculum, one that overlaps around the edges and is multifaceted, much like the magazine pictures we cut out and glued on pieces of cardboard when we were students. The following chapters comprise our collage, blur the edges, and reveal hiding places. Each chapter contains book titles that extend instruction. Recommendations of good children's literature and writing activities are provided throughout the book. All of the chapters embrace the notion of play as a model for learning, experimentation as a way of knowing, and language as a vehicle for moving in and out of subject-area domains. The book includes readings that spur writing, art, talk, and imaginative acts, and writings that encourage children to write personally, poetically, and "professionally."

In some ways, the book exemplifies Tom Romano's multigenre research paper, in which adolescent writers are encouraged to reinvent the traditional term paper by selecting material about a topic from multiple genres rather than from informational books only (Romano 1995). We aspire to the same goal. In fact, we hope to deconstruct the boundaries among disciplines as well as among genres and take Romano's work across the curriculum and into elementary and middle school classrooms. The edges of separate study instruction are blurred.

How to Use This Book

Because learning is a linking of ideas and experiences, no one starting point is right for all students or classes of students. The best teachers know their children and the content and skills they need to teach, and then work with their students to create study that encourages children to grow as readers, writers, and thinkers. The chapters in this book were approached from a number of different directions to show some of the possibilities for combining subjects, themes, and genres for study. What is included is not comprehensive, but instead shows one or more possible approaches to try. The index at the back of the book will help with the location of specific authors, titles, and subjects. In each section of the book are annotated lists of children's books that inform and support children's studies. Titles are followed by the designation (P) when they work well in primary (K–2) classrooms, (U) when they work well in upper elementary, or (U/P) when they work well for middle and upper elementary students. Of course, any picture book has the potential for modeling writing at all levels.

Chapter One, "Messing Around: Sharing the Writing Process with Our Favorite Authors," describes how children learn from the company they keep. We tell our own stories of unearthing writing and reading and offer ways of enlisting the help of children's authors. This chapter provides broad background on the writing process and how to link it with the works that children read.

Chapter Two, "Blurring the Edges Through a Thematic Unit on Mystery, Magic, and History," connects a popular literary genre with other literary study and social studies. We include a brief unit on riddles, fairy tales, and fantasies that feature magic, and a unit on the tall-tale magic in the works of Sid Fleischman.

Chapter Three, "Letters and Diaries as a Unifying Form Across the Disciplines," begins and ends with a personal letter to our readers. Because the study of letter writing and pen pals is popular in language arts, we try to show how this can be expanded to include literary study and other forms of writing for personal purposes. Units on informal and formal correspondence, holiday and special occasion correspondence are included. Because diaries and journals are a form of self-correspondence, modern and historical, fictional, and autobiographical examples are included.

Chapter Four, "Who's Counting?: Using Writing and Literature to Understand Mathematics," encompasses several popular topics in mathematics, including units on counting and numbers, teaching chronology as a link with social studies, and using language as a means of assessing mathematical competencies. Books that feature math concepts and attitudes toward mathematics are included.

Chapter Five, "Just Look: Observing the World Around Us as Scientists and Creative Writers," discusses the links among scientists, authors, and poets and the processes they use to observe and investigate the natural world. Unique ways of writing about science, units on the Big Dipper and on migration of geese, as well as writing activities using catalogues and questions are included.

Chapter Six, "Textures of Things," includes units on the sense of touch and on textures in art and food. A unit on rocks suggests that texture may provide a link among science, art, and language arts studies. Units on experiencing texture through our sense of touch and through the tastes and textures of foods are included. Textures you can see in picture books featuring quilts, collages, and other paper construction in their illustrations are discussed. Finally, we return to the notion of a collage curriculum by suggesting scrapbooks, which may help children tie together and blur the lines among aspects of their learning experiences.

We invite you to probe, ponder, and unearth what may be concealed in the ordinary places of your classrooms. As authors, we brainstormed hiding places and exchanged ideas about the subjects, blurring our separate thoughts. We came to believe more strongly in collaboration and communication as a means of understanding. We took two I's and created a collective *we*, the voice you hear on these pages. We ask you to join us in probing the notion of blurring the edges in your own classrooms as well.

around the classroom with signs that say "Discovery Drafts" or "First Attempts." Perhaps an explanation could accompany the label that makes its clear that discovery drafts represent writers' initial efforts at generating texts. Discovery drafts are fresh, "thinking-on-paper" drafts that are inherently unpolished.

Finished pieces may be published in books that are stacked on shelves among favorite authors or checked out from the school library. Revision can be featured by displaying actual drafts that have lines crossed out, arrows going everywhere, notes in the margin, and a sign that reads, "Make It Messy To Make It Clear."

Regardless of where they are in their writing processes, children need assistance. Assistance comes in the form of direct instruction, modeling, and conferencing, and from children teaching other children how to solve writing problems. Assistance also comes from children's books and children's authors who share their writing processes in their autobiographies.

Reading and Writing: A Collaboration with Children's Authors

Reading teacher Frank Smith said, "We learn to write from the company we keep" (Smith 1992, 432). Such company includes friends, families, and the authors we read. Children learn to write from Betsy Byars, Cynthia Rylant, Jane Yolen, Sid Fleischman, Paul Fleischman, and many others. Author Sid Fleischman acknowledged that the company he kept was an important part of his son's decision to become a writer. Fleischman explained, "In and out of our house came Maurice Sendak and Clyde Robert Bulla and Julia Cunningham and Bill Peet and the poet Myra Cohn Livingston. This literary company was to have an effect on Paul" (Fleischman 1996, 176).

As young writers keep company with authors and poets, they notice the techniques that are used. This borrowing of structures, language, and literary elements happens spontaneously with children in classrooms in which the structures and power of words are honored. For example, a third-grader who loved Karla Kuskin's prickly poem "Thistles" and had discussed the sounds of the words in the poem with Barbara, waved cheerfully to her as she left the room with her lunch buddy, calling out a phrase from the poem, "Goodbye. We're off to have a *lovely lunch*" (Kuskin 1980). In another classroom, a fourth-grade girl whose family was struggling with a divorce wrote a letter to Mr. Henshaw, the fictional character in Beverly Cleary's *Dear Mr.*

Henshaw. She told Barbara she knew he wasn't real, but she thought writing the letter might help her in the same way it helped the character, Leigh Botts. Encouraging children to study how their favorite authors craft stories and poems is instructive at two levels: the technique level and the writing process level.

In their autobiographies, some authors describe how they use the world around them to collect raw material for their books. They acknowledge that they have listened to other people's conversations, drawn from their childhood experiences, and gotten feedback from readers—family members, friends, and editors (O'Laughlin 1997). Sharing these stories with children illustrates the uniqueness of the writing process. Students may observe that one writer uses a jot list to get started, another starts with a list of possible titles for a novel, a third begins with a drawing, and a fourth starts with a family story handed down through generations.

Although authors differ in their writing processes, they also have much in common. For example, most authors claim to be avid readers. In fact, children's author, Avi states, "Unless you are a reader, you cannot become a writer. The more you read, the better your writing will be" (McClure & Kristo 1996, 213).

As more authors share their writing processes through their autobiographies, children may see that the writing process of a favorite author is similar to their own. When writing processes are compared in the classroom, students become aware of the unique nature of writing—the fact that it looks the same in some cases and different in others. Newbery Medal winner Patricia MacLachlan explained, in *Meet the Authors and Illustrators*, "There is no right way to write. Each writer must learn to bring out her voice in her own way" (Kovacs & Preller 1991, 117).

Author Autobiographies

Aardema, V. 1995. *A Bookworm Who Hatched.* Katonah, NY: Richard C. Owen. (P)

Asch, F. 1997. *One Man Show.* Katonah, NY: Richard C. Owen. (P)

Ashabranner, B. 1990. *The Times of My Life: A Memoir.* New York: Cobblehill. (U)

Bauer, M.D. 1995. *A Writer's Story: From Life to Fiction.* New York: Clarion. (U)

Bulla, C.R. 1985. *A Grain of Wheat.* New York: David R. Godine. (U)

Bunting, E. 1995. *Once Upon a Time.* Katonah, NY: Richard C. Owen. (P)

Byars, B. 1991. *The Moon and I*. Englewood Cliffs, NJ: Julian Messner. (U)

Cleary, B. 1988. *A Girl from Yamhill*. New York: Morrow. (U)

———. 1995. *My Own Two Feet*. New York: Avon Books. (U)

Cole, J., & W. Saul. 1996. *On the Bus with Joanna Cole*. Portsmouth, NH: Heinemann. (P)

Copeland, J.S., & V.L. Copeland. 1994. *Speaking of Poets 2: More Interviews with Poets Who Write for Children and Young Adults*. Urbana, IL: National Council of Teachers of English. (U)

Crews, D. 1991. *Bigmama's*. New York: Greenwillow. (P)

Dahl, R. 1984. *Boy: Tales of Childhood*. New York: Puffin. (U)

De Paola, T. 1989. *The Art Lesson*. New York: Putnam. (P)

Ehlert, L. 1997. *Hands*. San Diego: Harcourt Brace. (P)

———. 1996. *Under My Nose*. Katonah, NY: Richard C. Owen. (P)

Fleischman, S. 1996. *The Abracadabra Kid: A Writer's Life*. New York: Greenwillow. (U)

Fritz, J. 1982. *Homesick: My Own Story*. Illus. by Margot Tomes. New York: Putnam. (U)

———. 1985. *China Homecoming*. New York: Putnam. (U)

———. 1992. *Surprising Myself*. Katonah, NY: Richard C. Owen. (U)

Goble, P. 1994. *Hau Kola, Hello Friend*. Katonah, NY: Richard C. Owen. (P)

Greenfield, E., & L.J. Little. 1993. *Childtimes: A Three-Generation Memoir*. San Diego: Harcourt Brace. (U)

Heller, R. 1996. *Fine Lines*. Katonah, NY: Richard C. Owen. (P)

Hopkins, L. 1992. *The Writing Bug*. Katonah, NY: Richard C. Owen. (U)

Hurwitz, J. 1998. *A Dream Come True*. Katonah, NY: Richard C. Owen. (U/P)

Hyman, T. 1981/1989. *Self-Portrait: Trina Schart Hyman*. New York: HarperCollins. (U/P)

Joyce, W. 1997. *The World of William Joyce*. New York: HarperCollins. (U)

Kovacs, D., & J. Preller. 1991. *Meet the Authors and Illustrators*. New York: Scholastic. (U/P)

Kuskin, K. 1995. *Thoughts, Pictures, and Words*. Katonah, NY: Richard C. Owen. (U)

Lester, H. 1997. *Author: A True Story*. Boston: Houghton, Mifflin. (P)

Little, J. 1988. *Little by Little: A Writer's Education*. New York: Viking. (U)

London, J. 1998. *Tell Me a Story*. Katonah, NY: Richard C. Owen. (P)

Lyon, G.E. 1996. *A Wordful Child*. Katonah, NY: Richard C. Owen. (U/P)

Mahy, M. 1995. *My Mysterious World*. Katonah, NY: Richard C. Owen. (U)

Martin, R. 1992. *A Storyteller's Story*. Katonah, NY: Richard C. Owen. (U)

McKissack, P. 1997. *Can You Imagine?* Katonah, NY: Richard C. Owen. (P)

McPhail, D. 1996. *In Flight with David McPhail: A Creative Autobiography.* Portsmouth, NH: Heinemann. (P)

Naylor, P.R. 1987. *How I Came to Be a Writer.* New York: Simon & Schuster. (U)

Paterson, K. 1981. *The Gates of Excellence: On Reading and Writing Books for Children.* New York: Dutton. (U)

Paulsen, G. 1990. *Woodsong.* New York: Simon & Schuster. (U)

Peet, B. 1989. *Bill Peet: An Autobiography.* Boston: Houghton Mifflin. (U/P)

Polacco, P. 1994. *Firetalking.* Katonah, NY: Richard C. Owen. (P)

Pringle, L. 1997. *Nature! Wild and Wonderful.* Katonah, NY: Richard C. Owen. (U/P)

Ringgold, F. 1995. *We Flew over the Bridge: The Memoirs of Faith Ringgold.* Boston: Bulfinch Press. (U/P)

Ringgold, F., L. Freeman & N. Roucher. 1996. *Talking to Faith Ringgold.* New York: Crown. (U/P)

Rylant, C. 1987. *But I'll Be Back Again.* New York: Orchard. (U/P)

———. 1992. *Best Wishes.* Katonah, NY: Richard C. Owen. (U/P)

Stevenson, J. 1987. *Higher on the Door.* New York: Greenwillow. (U)

———. 1992. *Don't You Know There's a War On?* New York: Greenwillow. (U)

Uchida, Y. 1986. *When I Was Nine.* New York: Greenwillow. (U)

———. 1991. *The Invisible Thread.* New York: Simon & Schuster. (U)

Yep, L. 1991. *The Lost Garden.* New York: Simon & Schuster. (U)

Yolen, J. 1992. *A Letter from Phoenix Farm.* Katonah, NY: Richard C. Owen. (U/P)

The Writing Process

Prewriting

Prewriting includes choosing a potential topic to explore as well as gathering enough raw material to determine whether the subject merits further investigation. Often, choosing the topic is the most difficult part. It's important to take class time to talk about how writers find topics. By experimenting with the prewriting strategies suggested here, writers can determine whether they have the necessary interest and the potential "data" to develop a particular topic.

Many teachers have children keep lists of writing topics in their folders, adding to the lists as ideas strike. Sharing lists out loud triggers topics, reminding writers of potential subjects. Hobbies, sports, friends, family, pets, and subjects being studied in various classes often show up on children's "Things to Write About" lists.

Because writers write with information, not words (Murray 1996), children must find ways to gather material for their subjects. Some teachers brainstorm ideas with the entire class, creating group webs on colorful wall charts; others ask children to "jot list" about their topics in their notebooks, listing what they know about their subjects and what they need to find out. They often ask them to circle five or six items that seem most important. Probing memories, reflecting on past experiences, rereading letters, and leafing through scrapbooks and photo albums are discovery procedures that bring the writer's past into the present. Looking at oneself as a resource for information is the place to begin a piece of writing.

Another prewriting strategy is to involve others in the search for material about a particular topic, including interviews with family and friends as well as with subject-area experts. In addition, students may need to gather material from libraries, public institutions, and other agencies.

Children can learn about prewriting from their favorite authors. Teachers can read aloud sections from author autobiographies that explain how various writers get started on their own writing projects. For example, Betsy Byars believes, "Plenty of good scraps are as important in making a book as in making a quilt" (Byars 1991, 39). Byars calls her books scrapbooks because they contain interesting things she sees and hears when she listens to the radio, walks in the woods, reads a book, and visits the library—motions that she goes through to get started on her writing. Children's author Katherine Paterson expressed her feelings about getting started in the following statement, "After many false starts I began to write a story in pencil in a used spiral notebook, so that if it came to nothing, I could pretend that I'd never been very serious about it" (Paterson 1988, 62).

Young writers who appear in children's books also discuss strategies for getting started. For example, Anastasia Krupnik, in Lois Lowry's book by the same name (1979), fills her notebooks with lists of names, definitions of words she likes, and lists of people she likes or dislikes. Libby McCall, the young writer in Zilpha Keatley Snyder's *Libby On Wednesday* (1991), makes notes in journals designated for special tasks, including comments about books she is reading and current projects she is working on.

Besides modeling topic selection and prewriting strategies and sharing techniques of well-known authors, teachers can have an impact on this stage of writing simply by teaching it at the same time each day.

Because much of this *getting-started* stage takes place over time, and in the writer's head, knowing that writing time is provided on a regular basis allows the writer to think about her topic when she's not writing. Donald Graves calls this "rehearsal time" (Graves 1994). An idea for a piece of writing comes to a child on the playground or at home, and she thinks, "I'll write about that tomorrow during writing time!" Knowing that writing time is fixed keeps the ideas coming.

Prewriting also involves figuring out what to do with the scraps of information, jot lists, freewriting, notes, and outlines that are generated. Deciding what to include, and why (focus), determine the direction the writing will take.

Focus: Finding a Way "In"

Finding a focus is difficult for all writers. Trying to maintain that focus from prewriting to revision can be even more difficult. Some writers for children have attempted to walk through the drafts of their work to show young writers how they focus their pieces. Eve Merriam's "Writing a Poem," in her collection *A Sky Full of Poems*, for example, takes young writers through her first idea for a poem and its many revisions to the final focused piece (Merriam 1986, 91).

When teachers write with their students during writing times, they model the process in the same way they do during Sustained Silent Reading. In these following pages, Lynne shares her writing process for a piece on the death of her mother, a subject about which she struggles to write with focus and clarity. Her thoughts are interspersed with comments on her work with a group of sixth-graders and general comments about the writing process. Lynne explains her writing process:

> While I was freewriting with the students about my mother's death, I began to see a theme evolving. Lots of my writing related to food and to my mother preparing it. When I finished my free write, I circled the parts I liked best and wrote my mom a letter. At this point, I was surprised to find myself getting angry. I wrote, "How could you die when I still need you? How could you die on Christmas Eve?" Again, I circled the parts I liked, realizing that there were several stories emerging from my prewriting. Rereading the parts I circled, I decided to focus on cooking. I chose this focus for two reasons: First, I was writing this with students and knew I would be able to share a cooking piece (or at least parts of it) comfortably during the

After the minilesson on leads, the writers began to play around with words that would hook their readers' attention as well as direct it in the way they wanted. They experimented with three possible openings for their stories, including conversation, description, a flashback, a startling fact, a rhetorical question, a memory, or a picture in their minds that they wanted to capture in writing.

> In my first opening, I recalled a phone conversation I had with my mother, asking her for cooking advice. In my second opening, I described a scene in my mother's kitchen. My third began with the question, "How can I ever get along without you?" I decided to go with this one, having realized during my mother's illness just how much I relied on her when I was cooking. I've decided that my piece will begin, "I knew when my mother died, I would miss her most when I was baking."

The writers shared their leads with a partner. After sharing, Lynne asked, "How many of you heard an opening that made you want to hear more?" The students said they heard "great stuff" and encouraged their partners to keep writing.

At this point in the process, they had tentative titles, and possible leads, but the writers needed anecdotes, examples, and/or "word vignettes" to flesh out their most important points. Following writing teacher Donald Graves' suggestion in Donald Murray's *Writing to Learn* (1996), Lynne asked the students to reread the material they had circled during the prewriting activities. She asked them to put a "B" if they thought the circled information would work best toward the beginning of their pieces, an "M" if they thought it might fit best in the middle, and an "E" if the information seemed to belong toward the end.

> I identified three major ideas (sequences) from my circled items: the favorite recipes my mother prepared for each of my brothers and sisters (to go in the beginning of the piece); the warning from the heart doctor (to be discussed somewhere in the middle); and the Christmas Eve when my mother collapsed on the kitchen floor (to end the piece). I'm worried that if I tell too much about what happened on Christmas Eve, the ending will not reflect the beginning, and the piece will be out of focus.

It's Time to Write

At this point, the students and Lynne had focus statements, titles, openings, and several ideas (sequences) to use in their writing. After rereading the material, they put everything away. Lynne set the timer for thirty minutes, and everyone began to write. The goal was to write throughout the entire amount of time, including what they remembered from prewriting as well as anything new that came to mind. The task was to create a draft filled with ideas that could be added to, deleted, or rearranged during the revision stage.

The discovery drafts produced results: a surprise about a topic, a new direction for the piece, a signal that this might not be the right time to write about the subject. At this juncture, the writers weighed their options just like professional writers do, asking: Do I incorporate the new information and keep the same focus? Do I refocus the piece and return to the prewriting stage for new raw material? Do I put the draft away for the time being and choose another topic? They discussed how new information can enhance the main point, change the main point altogether, or cause them to abandon the subject, something Lynne encouraged the students to consider. She reminded them that writing, like cooking, gardening, and other natural events, has its time and occasion.

We want to pause here and draw your attention to the overlapping nature of the stages of writing. Learning does not follow the tidy linear sequences often described in lesson plans. At a literal level, prewriting implies a preliminary action that is used to begin the writing process. In reality, writers return to the prewriting stage throughout the writing process. We are in and out of all the stages of the writing process from beginning to end.

Revision

The students and Lynne began the revision process by reading their drafts out loud to partners (who stayed the same throughout the creation of the pieces). Lynne read a quote from Judy Blume to the students: "When you read aloud you can hear what doesn't work" (Kovacs & Preller 1991, 83).

A third-grader we know had a similar experience. She was reading aloud her story about a magic show when she paused and asked, "I wonder why I put in the part about my sister's clown costume?" She heard this line "jar" the text, and realized it needed to be deleted. When she omitted the line, the piece flowed. When Lynne asked about her revision, the young writer explained that between magic acts her little sister entertained the audience by being a clown. Because that part was not explained in the story, her decision to omit it contributed to the focus of her piece.

Revising Chunk by Chunk

After reading aloud, Lynne and the students decided to work as editors on one section of their drafts at a time. Borrowing the following kinds of questions from Murray (1996), they asked themselves the following: Does the title catch my reader's attention? Does it direct the piece? Do my opening lines do the same? Have I hooked my reader? Do the sequences I've used to develop my ideas fall in the correct places (i.e., in an order that is pleasing and understandable to others)? The writers tried to answer each question in regard to the main point they wanted to make and in regard to their readers. They reflected on whether they might have given too much information too quickly. Or too little. Lynne encouraged the students to experiment with moving the sequences of their pieces around to give their readers information at just the right time. She kept reminding them to "Make It Messy to Make It Clear."

Finally, having determined that their titles, openings, and sequences said what they wanted, the writers looked at the tentative endings they had generated earlier and asked themselves, "Does my ending resemble my beginning?" Lynne explained how the ending gives a sense of closure and is the final chance to echo the main point. One student's closing paragraph focused his piece beautifully. In fact, the class decided it made a better opening than an ending. Flip-flopping the paragraph improved the flow of the paper.

Other editing strategies that teachers and students might employ in a writing workshop include adding new information (more prewriting), experimenting with word choice and replacing trite words with fresh ones, substituting vague nouns with specific ones, and paying attention to the emotional effects our words might have on a reader. They might also put their drafts away for a brief period, like author Beverly Cleary, who sets her stories aside so she can view them with fresh eyes (Kovacs & Preller 1991, 86).

When the students and Lynne returned to their pieces, they were able to assess the potential impact of their words. They experimented with additional techniques, such as conveying meaning through showing instead of telling, adding detail, and replacing weak verbs with strong ones.

Proofreading: A Courtesy to Readers

When the students decided that the meaning of their stories was clear to them and to their partners, they were ready to proofread. Lynne explained that it is during the proofreading stage that the writer is concerned with correct spelling, punctuation, capitalization, and other "technical courtesies." She asked the students to read their edited drafts out loud to determine whether their pieces were punctuated correctly, pausing naturally at places in the texts that require pause marks, such as commas, semicolons, and end punctuation marks.

Early in the school year, the children had begun keeping a list of "Skills Learned," which Lynne used as a proofreading record sheet, stapling one to each draft. Pairs of students proofread a partner's work, using the record sheet as a guideline. After checking for mechanical errors such as capitalization, punctuation, and spelling, the proofreader signed the sheet, sharing some of the writer's responsibility for correctness. This benefited both the proofreader and the writer.

In addition to editing and proofreading instruction, the class learned about revision techniques from their favorite authors. When Lynne shared Katharine Paterson's notebook containing her original drafts of *Bridge to Terabithia*, it helped the students to realize that Paterson, like themselves, crossed out words, wrote comments in the margin, and used arrows to make revisions in her text (Paterson 1988).

Some of the students revised as they composed. Lynne shared revision strategies of a favorite author, Betsy Byars, to illustrate the idiosyncratic nature of the process: "By the time I finish my first draft, I've written between the lines and around the edges and on the back of the paper. It's a mess" (Byars 1991, 86). Byars' in-process revision was similar to several students' revision processes and confirmed for them that there were multiple ways to *work* a draft.

Some of the sixth-graders did their revision by hand; others used the computer; several did both. Revision was a favorite part of the writing process for many who agreed with Judy Blume's statement in *Meet the Authors and Illustrators* (Kovacs & Preller 1991, 82): "I'm a rewriter. That's the part I like best. I despise and am terrified by a first draft. But once I have a pile of paper to work with, it's like having the pieces of a puzzle. I just have to put the pieces together to make a picture."

Teachers may want to turn to characters in children's books to help students learn about revision. In Jane Yolen's *The Giants Go Camping*, the character of Little Dab spends a good deal of time revising a recipe he is writing. Little Dab uses a pencil to cross out and change the work in progress. Sid Fleischman's characters, Hold-Your-Nose-Billy and Cutter, with the help of Jemmy, revised a ransom note in *The Whipping Boy*. Some revision strategies may not deal specifically with writing but still show the importance of a revising process, such as Gregory's revisions of his art work in Cynthia Rylant's *All I See*.

Going Public

One way to publish student writing is through sharing it out loud. For Lynne's sharing session, chairs were pulled into a circle, treats were served, and the students took turns reading their polished pieces. They heard a variety of kinds of writing, including personal narratives, a collection of poems, and several short stories.

Sharing their final drafts in a formal setting motivated the students to keep writing. Having moved their audience with a humorous line, a tension-filled scene, or a poignant image, they realized the power of their words. They knew success when listeners howled with laughter or when the room became appropriately silent, and they were eager to write again. Reading their works aloud showed the "writerly" side of each student, a side that could easily have gone unnoticed. Through their shared processes and products, the writers felt connected. They were members of the literacy club (Smith 1986).

In considering the sharing session, Lynne made the decision not to read her entire piece to the students. She shared in the writing process, shared parts of every draft, and shared family stories. However, she was not comfortable sharing the piece in its entirety. Lynne reflected on her decision in the following journal entry:

> I'm done. I've written the piece. I loved working on it with the students, and it was a source of numerous "lessons." However, for the first time ever, I'm choosing not to share a whole piece with them. I explained to them how it felt more like a piece to share with my family, and I thanked them for their help. They seemed to understand. Who knows, they may make the same decision some time in their writing lives?

Other Ways to Publish Students' Writing

There are lots of other ways for children to share their writing formally and informally. The simplest way is to exhibit it in public places—hallways, cafeterias, and walls of classrooms. When a classroom is filled with student writing—early drafts, lists of possible topics, samples of various kinds of writing, student-made books, and proofreading charts—a clear signal is flashed to anyone who enters: "This is a place where writers are at work, and a writer's work is never done!"

In addition to displaying children's work in schools, we can bind their finished pieces and display them in medical offices or in local libraries. Published books can be shared with family members or given as gifts to loved ones. It's important to remember, however, that not everything needs to be published. It is the process of writing, as much as the product, that needs to be emphasized. The writer learns about herself and her world through the act of writing; making her insights public may or may not be necessary. Betsy Byars captured this sentiment when she described a manuscript she had written about a seven-day flight she made with her husband: "Well, after I finally, finally finished the manuscript and sent it to my publisher, they didn't like it. They said it didn't have enough plot construction. I've now written the manuscript approximately seventeen times, and it still doesn't have enough plot construction. I'm not discouraged. I may get it on the eighteenth try. And if it never gets published, I'm still glad we did it" (Byars 1991, 81). The joy for Byars was in the process: the collecting of two hundred pages of notes, her attempts to capture the flight on paper, and the flight itself. Byars' approach sends the important message that a process is not diminished by the lack of a published product.

Reading and Writing Across the Curriculum

The company that children keep on any given day is scintillating. The scientists, mathematicians, historians, poets, and artists they study are all exploring the world through language, inquiry, and speculation. Whether students are predicting the next event in a story or the outcome of a science experiment, they are using language to learn. Through oral, written, and visual representations, they make linkages to the world around them.

One of the ways we try to help students see these links is by creating thematic units in which we move across the fixed lines of the curriculum to explore ideas and perspectives. The following chapter demonstrates how one such possible unit might be created. This unit capitalizes on connections among literature and history, fact and fiction, and magic and realism as it guides students' exploration of the topic of mystery.

with a caption and story title, left with a publisher by an author who never comes back with the finished stories. One drawing, for example, shows a house rising up into the air, with rocket flames shooting out from beneath it, and is captioned, "It was a perfect liftoff." This and other eerie events have invited children to imagine the whole story behind each picture and to write that story for others to think about. Other picture book puzzles invite writings because they contain no words. What really does happen in the mysterious *The Grey Lady and the Strawberry Snatcher* or in Graeme Base's *The Eleventh Hour*? Perhaps the written explanation provided by young writers in the classroom will help us all to understand.

Picture Book Puzzles

Ahlberg, J. & A. Ahlberg. 1979. *Each Peach Pear Plum: An I Spy Story*. New York: Viking. (P)
Younger children can spy hidden Mother Goose characters on each page of this simple picture book.

Anno, M. 1983. *Anno's Mysterious Multiplying Jar*. New York: Philomel. (U)
In this deceptively simple book, pictures of everyday objects are used to explain factorials.

———. 1987. *Anno's Math Games*. New York: Philomel. (U)

———. 1989. *Anno's Math Games II*. New York: Philomel. (U)

———. 1991. *Anno's Math Games III*. New York: Philomel. (U)
Difficult math concepts are presented through pictures, diagrams, and games in these volumes.

Bang, M. 1980. *The Grey Lady and the Strawberry Snatcher*. New York: Four Winds. (P)
The Grey Lady "disappears" against the background of these pictures as she evades the Strawberry Snatcher.

Base, G. 1987. *Animalia*. New York: Abrams. (U/P)
An alliterative phrase and a picture full of animals and objects to identify are provided for each letter in this complex alphabet book.

———. 1989. *The Eleventh Hour*. New York: Abrams. (U)
An elaborate mystery involving a gala party can be solved through careful study of these illustrations.

Macaulay, D. 1990. *Black and White*. Boston: Houghton Mifflin. (U)
Several stories intertwine in this wordless book puzzle for older students.

McPhail, D. 1984. *Fix-it*. New York: Dutton. (P)

The title pages in this small book give clues to solve the mystery of the broken television.

Maisner, H. 1995. *The Magic Globe: An Around the World Adventure Game.* Illus. by A. Baron. Cambridge, MA: Candlewick. (U)

Children may choose their adventure in this book that leads them on a globe-trotting journey that teaches geography along the way.

_____. 1994. *The Magic Hourglass: A Time Travel Adventure Game.* Illus. by P. Joyce. Cambridge, MA: Candlewick. (U)

This volume allows readers to choose from several adventures as they travel back through the centuries to revisit history.

Martin, B., Jr. 1964/1992. *Brown Bear, Brown Bear, What Do You See?* Illus. by E. Carle. New York: Holt. (P)

_____. 1991. *Polar Bear, Polar Bear, What Do You Hear?* Illus. by E. Carle. New York: Holt. (P)

Young children can predict what will be seen or heard next in these two picture books featuring clues to help the reader guess.

Sendak, M. 1981. *Outside Over There.* New York: HarperCollins. (U/P)

Ida falls backwards out the window to rescue her brother from the goblins in this mysterious story.

Talbott, J. 1994. *It's for You: An Amazing Picture-Puzzle Book.* New York: Dutton. (U)

A mysterious package leads the reader from one puzzle to another in this book that includes arithmetic riddles and rhymes.

Van Allsburg, C. 1984. *The Mysteries of Harris Burdick.* Boston: Houghton Mifflin. (U/P)

See text.

_____. 1986. *The Stranger.* Boston: Houghton Mifflin. (U/P)

A strange person, who might be Jack Frost, visits a farm in the autumn.

_____. 1991. *The Wretched Stone.* Boston: Houghton Mifflin. (U/P)

The crew of a sailing ship finds a magical stone that, with its mesmerizing properties, puts them all in peril.

Riddles

Another type of small mystery that elementary children enjoy is the language mystery found in riddles. Riddles capitalize on the homonyms and double meanings of our language in the way that puns do in jokes and metaphor does in poetry. In each riddle, as in poetry, one thing is described as if it is another. Poets have capitalized on the riddle by offering collections of riddles in poetic form. Charles Ghigna, for example, has asked what the lonely room might be (the hall) and who an invisible friend could be (the wind) in *Riddle Rhymes*, a collection for younger students. For upper elementary students, Brian Swann's *Touching the Distance: Native American Riddle Poems* uses much more complex riddles in both poems and art. Students at all grade levels may want to try their hand at writing their own poetic riddles.

███████████

Riddles

Corwin, J.H. 1998. *My First Riddles*. New York: HarperCollins. (P)
Very simple riddles that can be solved by young children involve everyday objects.

Ghigna, C. 1995. *Riddle Rhymes*. Illus. by J. Gorton. New York: Hyperion. (P)
See text.

Marzollo, J. 1998. *I Am a Rock*. Illus. by J. Moffatt. New York: Scholastic. (U/P)
Question-and-answer riddles about common rocks, and minerals such as salt, talc, coal, and so on, allow connections to science study in this book.

———. 1992. *I Spy: A Book of Picture Riddles*. Illus. by W. Wick. New York: Scholastic. (P)
Children are encouraged to find various everyday items from among many in this rhyming book that features photographs.

Nims, B.L. 1992. *Just Beyond Reach and Other Riddle Poems*. Illus. by G. Ancona. New York: Scholastic. (P)
A simple poem riddle is followed on the next page by a photograph that reveals the answer.

Spires, E. 1995. *With One White Wing: Puzzles in Poems and Pictures*. Illus. by E. Blegvad. New York: McElderry. (P)
Simple rhymed and unrhymed riddles are illustrated with pictures containing clues to their answers, which also appear upside down on the bottom of each page.

Swann, B. 1998a. *The House with No Door: African Riddle-Poems*. Illus. by A. Bryan. San Diego: Harcourt Brace. (U/P)
Simple riddles are illustrated with paintings that contain clues to their meanings.

———. 1998b. *Touching the Distance: Native American Riddle Poems*. Illus. by M. Rendon. San Diego: Browndeer/Harcourt Brace. (P)
See text.

███████████

Mystery Novels

If we and our students were given the task of defining what a mystery novel looked like, we might include some of the following items:

- The story has an exciting beginning. Something strange or terrible happens at the beginning of the story that makes us want to keep reading to find out what happens.
- That event creates a problem or mystery to be solved.
- There are a series of clues given to the reader so that he or she can try to solve the mystery along with the characters.
- Sometimes there are false clues or lies told or trails that go nowhere. Readers have to figure out what is true and what is just there to lead them away from the truth.
- The story concludes (usually) with the reader finding out whether his or her guesses were correct.

One of the things your students might do is to think about the books they have read and enjoyed over the past several years and list all the books they think have a *mystery* in them. Once they have a list of mysteries, they can sort their lists into categories. One group of fourth-graders included their favorite series mysteries, such as those by Stine and Martin, the Encyclopedia Brown detective novels, and the Nancy Drew books. They then considered that some of these mysteries included ghosts or eerie events, while others involved crimes committed in realistic settings. They noticed that sometimes the story was set in a mysterious place. Their teacher had read them Virginia Hamilton's *The House of Dies Drear*, about a house that once was a station on the underground railroad. The novel had the ghostly feel of a place where events in the past were still felt by the people who lived there in the present. Natalie Babbitt's *Tuck Everlasting*, in which water with mysterious powers flows from a brook in the woods outside of town, suggests that some places are magical, holding the secrets of time and eternity.

The fourth-graders brainstormed mysterious places they knew about or had visited as they thought about settings for their own mystery writings. Their first ideas were more prosaic—they included theme parks and Halloween horror houses where events had been contrived to scare them. Then, as they thought more deeply, students began to describe the hayloft of the barn at night, the trunk of old clothes in the basement, or the ancient petroglyphs of the Southwest. Their mystery writings began to include mysteries created from their own imaginative re-action to the spirits of the places they had experienced.

Some mysteries, the fourth-graders realized, happen because people are keeping secrets from one another; others because the major character stumbles into secretive events. Some of them had enjoyed Jean Craighead George's series of environmental mysteries, in which young people discover something wrong in the environment and trace back the mystery to find out how it could have happened. Besides mysteries with secrets and environmental mysteries, the students remembered disappearances and mysterious objects or games in mysteries they had read.

Within these and other categories, the students saw themes emerging. They described some mysteries as being more realistic. These could be solved by applying facts and reason to a situation to discover that what seemed an impossible mystery had a logical explanation, as happens in many detective stories. Others began to seem more unrealistic as the fourth-graders continued to read. R.L Stine's books often had terrifying and weird events described on their covers and in the opening chapters, but were generally solved as mere misunderstandings or dreams. The fourth-graders tried writing stories as they continued to read and expand their definitions of mysteries. No longer limiting themselves to one predictable form, they drew settings, characters, and mysteries from many sources.

Mystery Novels

Mysterious Places

Babbitt, N. 1975. *Tuck Everlasting.* New York: Farrar Straus Giroux. (U)
See text.

Hamilton, V. 1984. *The House of Dies Drear.* New York: Macmillan. (U)
See text.

Hobbs, W. 1995. *Kokopelli's Flute.* New York: Atheneum. (U)
A boy discovers a magical place in Southwestern ruins that helps him solve a mystery of thefts of historical artifacts.

Juster, N. 1961. *The Phantom Tollbooth.* Illus. by J. Feiffer. New York: Random House. (U)
An enchanted tollbooth takes a boy to magical worlds of numbers.

Wrightson, P. 1986. *The Nargun and the Stars.* New York: McElderry. (U)
A boy and his grandfather try to stop the destruction caused by the

slowly moving Nargun, an immense stonelike creature moving across the Australian landscape.

Other Mysteries

Avi. 1991. *The Man Who Was Poe*. New York: Avon. (U)
Two children who have been separated from their mother are helped by a strange man who turns out to be Edgar Allen Poe.

_____. 1990. *The True Confessions of Charlotte Doyle*. New York: Orchard. (U)
A girl crossing the Atlantic alone becomes involved in a mutiny.

Creech, S. 1994. *Walk Two Moons*. New York: HarperCollins. (U)
A girl searches for her mother, who abandoned the family years before.

George, J.C. 1991. *Who Really Killed Cock Robin?* New York: HarperCollins. (U)
See text.

_____. 1992. *The Missing 'Gator of Gumbo Limbo*. New York: HarperCollins. (U)

_____. 1993. *The Fire Bug Connection: An Environmental Mystery*. New York: HarperCollins. (U)

_____. 1996. *The Case of the Missing Cutthroats*. New York: HarperCollins. (U)

Konigsburg, E.L. 1967. *From the Mixed-Up Files of Mrs. Basil E. Frankweiler*. New York: Macmillan. (U)
In this classic book, two children who have run away to the Metropolitan Museum attempt to solve the mystery of an angel sculpture that was perhaps carved by Michelangelo.

Paterson, K. 1996. *Jip: His Story*. New York: Dutton. (U)
A boy, found as an infant fallen from a cart, lives in an asylum with a strange sad man and attempts to locate the mother he lost.

Pearce, P. 1983. *The Way to Sattin Shore*. Illus. by C. Voake. New York: Greenwillow. (U)
A girl seeks to find out what happened to her father, who disappeared on the day she was born.

Raskin, E. 1978. *The Westing Game*. New York: Dutton. (U)
This complex but lighthearted mystery involving chess and the words to "America the Beautiful" has been a favorite of upper level readers since it was published.

Snyder, Z.K. 1986. *The Egypt Game*. New York: Dell. (U)
A game played by six girls is interrupted when one of the players is attacked and a neighborhood child is murdered.

In this traditional Algonquin story, a young girl whose face and hands have been scarred by fire is the only one who can actually see the invisible being who many in the village, including her two wicked sisters, want to marry.

Perrault, C. 1971. *Cinderella*. Illus. by M. Brown. New York: Simon & Schuster. (P)

This best-known version of the Cinderella story features magic and a kind princess who forgives her tormentors.

Wheeler, P. 1989. *Vasilissa the Beautiful*. Memphis: Creative Press. (P)

With the help of a doll given to her by her mother before her death, beautiful Vassilisa is able to fend off her stepsisters and an evil witch in this Russian folk tale that includes aspects of both the Cinderella and Hansel and Gretel fairy tales.

Yorinks, A. 1990. *Ugh!* Illus. by R. Egielski. New York: Farrar, Straus & Giroux. (P)

A fantasy involving a cave boy who is rescued through the invention of a Stone Age bicycle; this is a very different version of the classic story.

Magic Objects

Baker, K. 1989. *The Magic Fan*. San Diego: Harcourt Brace. (P)

Yoshi, a young builder uses a magic fan as inspiration to help save his village and discovers his own talents along the way.

De Paola, T. 1975. *Strega Nona*. New York: Prentice Hall. (P)

A kindly witch chastises Big Anthony for misusing her magic pot in this traditional Italian tale.

Grimm Brothers. 1974. *Snow White*. Illus. by T.S. Hyman. Boston: Little, Brown. (P)

The magic mirror tells the truth to Snow White's wicked stepmother in this traditional German story.

Lattimore, D.N. 1995. "Aladdin." In *Arabian Nights: Three Tales*. New York: HarperCollins. (P)

A magic carpet and magical lamp are magic objects included in these traditional middle Eastern tales.

Steig, W. 1976. *The Amazing Bone*. New York: Farrar, Straus & Giroux. (P)

See text.

Stevenson, R.L. 1996. *The Bottle Imp*. New York: Clarion. (P)

This modern fantasy, set in the South Seas, features a genie like that in *Aladdin*.

Modern Magicians: Sid Fleischman's Magic

The magical person with a magic object exists not only in literature, but also in modern entertainment. David Copperfield and Penn and Teller are popular entertainers who create sleight of hand, escapes, and tricks in the tradition of the ancient magicians. A thematic unit on mysteries might just as easily begin with student interest in magic tricks and how they work, rather than mystery stories. One entry into this aspect of the unit on mystery is through Newbery award–winning author Sid Fleischman, a writer of stories who is himself a magician.

Sid Fleischman decided to become a magician in the fifth grade. From library books, he learned sleight-of-hand tricks, and took his show on the road when he was fourteen. As a storyteller, a novelist, and a screenwriter, Fleischman probed the mysteries in the oral tradition and the mystery of the written word. His autobiography for children, *The Abracadabra Kid* (1996), embodies both. Students who read Fleischman's book will discover that he connected to reading and writing through his love of magic. He pored over books of tricks, played with language, and used the magician's performance as he began to write. As students read Fleischman's autobiography and some of his novels, they can see for themselves how magic infused his works. Some of Fleischman's stories involve figures full of conniving and tricks, as in *Chancy and the Grand Rascal* and *The Whipping Boy*. In *Mr. Mysterious and Company*, the main character is a magician.

The McBroom stories are tall tales about magical events like the day it snowed popcorn and the big wind that brought wolves rolling from the north like tumbleweeds. The tall tale is a particularly American form of literature that young writers might want to try. If they look at Steven Kellogg's humorous versions of tall tales, they may find ideas for exaggerating places and people they have visited or read about. Other tall tales involve heroic figures such as John Henry and can supply students with background on people who were larger than life. Sid Fleischman's books provide young writers with a variety of ways to think about magic and mystery in their own works.

Magical Books

Sid Fleischman's Magic

Fleischman, S. 1986. *The Whipping Boy.* New York: Greenwillow. (U)
   Prince Brat and his whipping boy, Jemmy, who takes all of his punishments for him, are forced to change roles when outlaws capture them.

_____. 1987. *The Scarebird*. New York: Greenwillow. (U/P)
A farmer gives his scarecrow a head and causes a series of surprising events.

_____. 1988. *By the Great Horn Spoon*. Illus. by E. Von Schmidt. Boston: Little, Brown. (U/P)
An orphan boy and his butler become involved in the California Gold Rush.

_____. 1989a. *Chancy and the Grand Rascal*. New York: Greenwillow. (U/P)
A boy and sly uncle outwit outlaws, misers, and scoundrels.

_____. 1989b. *The Ghost in the Noonday Sun*. New York: Greenwillow. (U/P)
A shanghaied boy gets involved with pirates.

_____. 1990. *The Midnight Horse*. New York: Greenwillow. (U)
Touch, a young boy, receives help from a magician ghost when he confronts a host of foes, including a thief.

_____. 1992a. *Here Comes McBroom*. New York: Greenwillow. (U/P)
A collection of all of the McBroom tales.

_____. 1992b. *McBroom's Wonderful One Acre Farm*. New York: Greenwillow. (P)
Three tall tales describe the adventures of Josh McBroom and his challenges on the farm.

_____. 1995. *The Thirteenth Floor*. New York: Greenwillow. (U)
Orphan Buddy Stebbins discovers that the thirteenth floor of an old building is a way to go back in time and soon finds himself on a pirate ship that is sinking.

_____. 1997. *Mr. Mysterious and Company*. New York: Greenwillow. (U/P)
The cast of a traveling magic show in the 1880s encounters a series of adventures.

Tall Tales

Kellogg, S. 1986a. *Paul Bunyan*. New York: Morrow. (P)
The huge logger and his blue ox, Babe, help reshape the American landscape from their home in Minnesota.

_____. 1986b. *Pecos Bill*. New York: Morrow. (P)
The cowboy hero of the Southwest creates the Great Salt Lake and the Grand Canyon with his daring deeds.

_____. 1992. *Mike Fink*. New York: Morrow. (P)
America's most famous flat boatman outshines all others as he works on the Mississippi River.

_____. 1995. *Sally Ann Thunder Ann Whirlwind Crockett*. New York: Morrow.
Sally Ann, the wife of Davy Crockett, fears nothing and proves it when Mike Fink tries to scare her.

Lester, J. 1994. *John Henry*. Illus. by J. Pinkney. New York: Dial. (P)
   John Henry challenges the new steel-driving machine to a contest in this
   story of life on the railroad in the nineteenth century.
Osborne, M.P. 1991. *American Tall Tales*. Illus. by M. McCurdy. New York:
   Knopf. (P)
   A collection that features a variety of tall tale heroes and heroines.
San Souci, R. 1993. *Cut from the Same Cloth: American Women of Myth, Leg-
   end, and Tall Tale*. Illus. by B. Pinkney. New York: Philomel. (P)
   This collection of stories includes mythical American women with super
   strengths and skills.

Exploring Mysteries of the Past Through Literature

Ancient people often found magical explanations for events they could not understand, and these have lived on in our literature. Modern writers of mysteries sometimes use magic and the mystery genre as a means of allowing readers to explore the past. Authors of fantasy novels, such as Sid Fleischman, have acknowledged that the past is rich with mysteries. Restless spirits and time shifts that allow us to go back in time to experience strange encounters with mysterious places and artifacts suggest that the past has an enormous hold over the present. History is full of mysterious events. Children enjoy speculating, as paleontologists do, about what happened to dinosaurs. These huge creatures still, as poet Valerie Worth has suggested, "walk around in everybody's heads." When they are approached as mysteries, stories of the past are fascinating to students. Why and how did people build the huge stone monoliths found at Stonehenge and other places around the world? How and why did people build the pyramids? What are the secrets of the Indian mounds found in eastern North America? What happened to the Anasazi people of the Southwest who disappeared, leaving their cliffside dwellings and possessions behind? Who were the sophisticated and violent people who lived in ancient Mexico? Each of these mysteries asks the questions basic to historical research: Why did people of certain places and times make the decisions they did, and what were the consequences of their choices?

   In some cases, the events of the past are truly mysterious because we have little recorded evidence for the events that happened. It is particularly important that students understand that much of what we know of these ancient people and their cultures is speculative and changes as new evidence is unearthed. Students will need to examine a variety of types of literary evidence of the past for which we have less clear historical documentation to see the different ways that historians, anthropologists, novelists, and poets seek to explain them. Sometimes, because factual, historical information about what actually occurred cannot be provided, an author chooses to explore the mystery through fiction. Novelists have tried to write about the lives of ancient people who lived before written language recorded their stories, fleshing out their lives through imagination and speculation. Poetry can capture the mysteries of past times when nothing is left but a feeling for a place. Joseph Bruchac's *Between Earth and Sky: Legends of Native American Sacred Places* and Jane Yolen's *Sacred Places* contain poems about places that hold an eerie power for modern people, just as they did for people in the past.

Informational books give us another view of these mysteries. Mike Corbishley's *Detecting the Past* contains brief overviews of fossils, bones, pollen, and mysteries about climate changes. Archaeological evidence such as pottery, standing stones, cave paintings, pictographs, tombs, and mummies is also described. Students' interest in mysteries of the past may also be piqued by museum visits, visits to historic or archaeological sites, and visual representations of early artistic endeavors, and through science activities.

Exploring Mysteries of the Past Through Literature

Ancient Egypt

Bunting, E. 1997. *I Am the Mummy: Heb-Nefert*. San Diego: Harcourt Brace. (U)

Told from the point of view of a long-dead Egyptian queen, this fictional picture book gives insights into the world of ancient Egypt.

Giblin, J.C. 1990. *The Riddle of the Rosetta Stone*. New York: Crowell. (U)

This is a nonfiction account of the discovery of the Rosetta stone and efforts to translate the languages cut into its surface.

Lattimore, D.N. 1992. *The Winged Cat: A Tale of Ancient Egypt*. New York: HarperCollins. (U/P)

The author–illustrator of this picture book tale uses hieroglyphs, narrative, and artistic motifs so that readers can help an Egyptian girl determine who caused the death of her cat.

Macaulay, D. 1975. *Pyramid*. Boston: Houghton Mifflin. (U)
   Macaulay's history uses line illustrations and a narrative of a fictional pharaoh to describe the building of a pyramid.

McGraw, E. 1985. *Mara, Daughter of the Nile*. New York: Puffin. (U)
   Mara, a mistreated slave, is given the opportunity to live in luxury when both king and queen want her to act as a spy in this historical novel.

———. 1986. *The Golden Goblet*. New York: Puffin. (U)
   Ronofer, a young Egyptian boy, longs to be a goldsmith but finds himself the apprentice to a cruel stonesmith instead.

Sabuda, R. 1994. *Tutankhamen's Gift*. New York: Simon & Schuster. (P)
   This is a picture book biography of the boy who became Pharaoh at age ten and built more monuments and temples to the old gods than any other pharaoh.

Trumble, K. 1996. *Cat Mummies*. Boston: Houghton Mifflin. (U/P)
   Focusing on cat mummies, this picture book explores the beliefs, history, and modern studies of the people of ancient Egypt.

The Aztecs

Bierhorst, J. 1993. *The Hungry Woman: Myths and Legends of the Aztecs*. New York: Morrow. (U/P)
   A folklorist shares stories told by contemporary Aztec people and includes paintings that show how these stories were preserved by ancient tellers.

Helly, M. & R. Courgeon. 1996. *Montezuma and the Aztecs*. New York: Holt. (U)
   A heavily illustrated encyclopedia, this shows the contributions of the Aztecs and their Spanish conquerors to modern Mexican culture.

Lattimore, D.N. 1987. *The Flame of Peace*. New York: HarperCollins. (U/P)
   Lattimore uses motifs from Aztec art and writing in this story that captures life in Aztec times.

Mason, A. 1997. *Aztec Times*. New York: Simon & Schuster. (U)
   An exploration of Aztec culture through text and pictures, this book also contains a fold-out time line and game board.

McDermott, G. 1997. *Musicians of the Sun*. New York: Simon & Schuster. (U/P)
   A retelling of an Aztec myth, in which wind frees four musicians from the sun so they can provide the world with music, this book is illustrated with motifs from Aztec art.

Wisiniewski, D. 1991. *Rain Player*. Boston: Houghton Mifflin. (P)
   Young Pik challenges the rain god to a game of pok-a-tok in order to bring water to his parched village.

Wood, T. 1992. *The Aztecs*. New York: Viking. (U)

This history of the Aztecs includes see-through scenes so that students can view both interiors and exteriors of buildings and religious structures.

Standing Stones

Hunter, M. 1996. *The Walking Stones*. San Diego: Harcourt Brace. (U)

Set in Scotland, this fantasy weaves together legends of the ancient Druids and their standing stones with a modern story about change.

Lyon, N. 1983. *The Mystery of Stonehenge*. Chatham, NJ: Raintree/Steck-Vaughan. (U)

This volume examines the theories that have existed throughout the years to explain the mystery of Stonehenge.

Roop, P. & C. Roop. 1989. *Stonehenge: Opposing Viewpoints*. San Diego: Greenhaven. (U)

The authors discuss different theories as to the meaning and purpose of the Stonehenge formations.

Yolen, J. 1996. "Stonehenge." In *Sacred Places*. San Diego: Harcourt Brace. (U)

A poem captures the sense of mystery surrounding the stones by posing a series of questions about those who might have erected them.

Zindel, P. 1995. *Doom Stone*. New York: HarperCollins. (U)

Young Jackson must travel to Stonehenge to unravel the mystery of a horrible beast threatening his Aunt Sarah.

The Anasazi

Bruchac, J. 1996. ". . . No One Lives Today . . ." In *Between Earth and Sky: Legends of Native American Sacred Places*. San Diego: Harcourt Brace. (U)

This selection tells of Native American people working together for the common good, and what can happen when one lusts for power.

Dewey, J.O. 1996. *Stories on Stone: Rock Art Images from the Ancient Ones*. Boston: Little, Brown. (U)

Using images from petroglyphs, Dewey explores the mystery of the people of the Southwest who disappeared.

Fisher, L.E. 1997. *Anasazi*. New York: Atheneum. (U/P)

This picture book describes the day-to-day life of the Anasazi people as it has been pieced together from artifacts.

Goodman, S.E. 1998. *Stones, Bones, and Petroglyphs: Digging into Southwest Archaeology*. Illus. by M.J. Doolittle. New York: Atheneum. (U)

Photographs of young people participating in archaeological digs and of artifacts are combined with text that explores the lives of the ancients.

Guiberson, B.Z. 1998. "The Disappearance of the Anasazi People." In

Mummy Mysteries: Tales from North America. New York: Holt. (U)

> The author discusses not only the mummified remains of the Anasazi, but also a number of other mummified remains found across the American continent in this simple chapter book that can be read by third- and fourth-graders interested in mysteries.

Hobbs, W. 1995. *Kokopelli's Flute*. New York: Atheneum. (U)

> By blowing on an ancient flute he finds in a cliff dwelling in the Southwest, Tep Jones opens a world of ancient magic in this fantasy novel that speculates on the lives of ancient Anasazi.

Exploring the Past Through Varying Perspectives

Children's books allow us to see the past through a variety of lenses. Although we tend to believe that history is fixed, it is continually changing. As our world changes and we as individuals change, we interpret and reinterpret the events of the past in different ways. What we understood about an event in our childhood has an entirely different meaning as we grow older and have children ourselves. Similarly, books of history and historical fiction change to reflect the understandings of new times. When Esther Forbes wrote *Johnny Tremain* (1943) at the height of patriotic fervor during World War II, she created a novel about the American Revolution that showed a strong, vibrant, emerging American people. When the Colliers wrote *My Brother Sam is Dead* (1984) after the unrest of the Vietnam War, their view was of a situation far more tragic and divisive. These writers viewed historical events, as both novelists and historians do, through the lenses of their own time period and understandings.

Perspectives on the Japanese-American Internment Camps

If we choose to study the mysteries of the past with our students, we also might try to explore them through a variety of lenses. How does a historian describe a particular event? A novelist? An artist? A poet? In a sense, the past is always mysterious to people who were not alive at a given time. Historians ponder such questions as how Thomas Jefferson, who wrote some of our most powerful documents on liberty, could have also kept slaves. How could people have mistreated others so horribly, as they have done through slavery, violence, and war, over time? To see how these lenses might function as we explore these mysteries of human nature, students could look at Yoshiko Uchida's books about the Japanese-American internment camps in which she was imprisoned as a child. Uchida wrote in the form of novels, picture books, autobiographical works, and letters as she tried to make sense, for herself and for others, of these life-changing events. Children who respond to Uchida's books and her plea not to forget injustices done to one another might also read nonfiction books, filled with photographs and personal stories, that can enrich their understandings of this event. They can look at other picture books that give small images of life in the camps and consequences for those who were imprisoned. As children read from a variety of genres, ideas are provided about how best to express their own ideas and feelings about events of the past, through factual portraits, fiction, letters, or poems.

The Japanese-American Internment Camps

Bunting, E. 1998. *So Far from the Sea*. Illus. by C.K. Soentpiet. New York: Clarion. (U/P)

In this picture book, a little girl and her family visit her grandfather's grave at Manzanar and share memories of life in the camp.

Hamanaka, S. 1990. *The Journey*. New York: Orchard. (U)

A photo essay featuring Hamanaka's mural of events surrounding the internment is an unflinching look at this period of history.

Means, F.C. 1993. *The Moved-Outers*. New York: Walker. (U)

One of the few novels written close to the actual period of the internment, this Newbery Medal book was first published in 1945.

Mochizuki, K. 1993. *Baseball Saved Us*. Illus. by D. Lee. New York: Lee and Low. (P)

A young boy perfects his baseball skills when his family is interned, and this helps him to make friends when he returns home.

Stanley, J. 1994. *I Am an American: The True Story of the Japanese Internment*. New York: Crown. (U/P)

This book uses interviews and personal recollections to tell the story of Shi Nomura, a high school senior sent to Manzanar relocation camp.

Tunnel, M. & G.W. Chilcott. 1996. *The Children of Topaz: The Story of a Japanese-American Internment Camp Based on a Classroom Diary*. New York: Holiday. (U)

A teacher's diary of life with children in the Utah camp forms the basis for this nonfiction exploration of children's lives.

Uchida, Y. 1993. *The Bracelet*. Illus. by J. Yardley. New York: Putnam. (U)

In this picture book for younger students, a young girl is comforted by the bracelet given her by a friend when her family is forced to leave home.

_____. 1991. *The Invisible Thread*. Englewood Cliffs, NJ: Messner. (U)

Uchida's autobiography describes her life before and during internment and the impact of the events on her and her family.

_____. 1978. *Journey Home*. New York: McElderry. (U)

This is a fictionalized retelling of Uchida's family's return to California to discover that most of their belongings have been stolen or sold.

_____. 1985. *Journey to Topaz*. San Francisco: Creative Arts. (U)

This is a fictionalized retelling of Uchida's family's move to and life in the Utah camp.

_____. 1990. "Letter from a Concentration Camp." In *The Big Book for Peace*, ed. A. Durrell & M. Sachs. New York: Dutton. (U)

A fictional letter from a boy interned at Tanforan to his friend at home in California describes the conditions and emotions at the horse stables-turned-housing.

Perspectives on Slavery

As social studies and literature curricula expand to include more voices, the perspectives of people from many sides of an issue help children to see history through another type of lens. As an example, a look at some of the growing number of books on slavery in the United States shows us that not only different genres of writing, but also different voices and perspectives can be introduced in historical study. How does our perspective of slavery change as we read historical fiction written from the point of view of insiders or sympathetic outsiders? Paula Fox's *The Slave Dancer*, a 1982 Newbery award–winning book, came under criticism because it was told from the perspective of a white cabin boy on a slave ship who helplessly watched the treatment of African people, who are portrayed as passive and submissive. More recent books present the horror of these events from the perspective of the slaves themselves. James Berry's *Ajeemah and His Son* is told from the perspective of a father and son captured in Africa by slave traders and shipped in chains to work on sugar cane plantations in Jamaica, and Joyce Hanson's *The Captive* is taken from events described in two slave narratives. Some books tell stories of sympathetic white Northerners who aided runaway slaves, while others capture these same experiences from the perspective of the runaway.

- What time period do I want to write about? Should I use descriptive language, poetic language, illustrations, or all of these to capture the time and place?
- What person or people do I want to write about? Who will be the major figures in my writing? How can I find out about what they were like and what their daily lives were like?
- Whose perspective would I like to write from? Who would best tell this story: an insider or an outsider? Someone from the time period? Should I use an historical or a modern perspective?
- How could I best tell about this history: through letters, diary or journal entries, poetry, or nonfiction prose? Perhaps some of each?

While studying historical evidence, students can also view events through the lenses that novelists, poets, storytellers, and artists have given us for understanding the people of a place and a time. As they read and observe and think about history, students begin to sort their thinking as historians do: What do we absolutely know from the evidence at this point in time? What do stories from the past reveal about how people lived and what they believed? What do poets and novelists tell us about how human beings are alike, even though they lived in different times and places? How do modern artists use the styles and designs of past artists to tell their stories to us? In essence, we begin to ask ourselves, "What are the facts?" and perhaps a somewhat different question, "What is the truth?"

Present or past, mysteries abound in the world around us. From picture book puzzles to riddles, from mysterious places to mysterious objects, the topic enthralls. Because they allow us to look at ways readers and writers have thought about and created mysteries, literature and history are the focus of study in this unit. It is not necessary to follow the flow of subjects we considered in this chapter or to include all of the parts of our unit in your studies. Any two mysteries may be linked when young readers and writers put together the pieces of their own puzzles. Readings of Sid Fleischman's books may pique children's interest in tall tales or lead to further study of magic. Collections of picture books might be thought of as puzzles but might also open doors to art activities. Enjoyment of the collections of riddle poems may lead to explorations and creation of other riddles, or to further poetry study. Puzzling questions might lead us to discover mysteries in math and science, and music and health as well. Mysteries and mysterious events lure us into learning—into predicting, problem solving, and inquiry. They provide a vehicle for thematic study, because curiosity and wonder naturally move across discipline lines.

A special type of gift letter is the birth letter. Many baby books contain pages for parents to write letters to their newborns. Birth letters are timeless gifts written in anticipation of a birth or in the desire to begin a new, long-term relationship. An example of this is found in Judith Caseley's children's book, *Dear Annie*, in which letters and postcards are exchanged between a loving grandfather and a child from the time of her birth. Several picture books read like birth letters to a child, although they are not set up in strict letter format. Deborah Frazier's *On the Day You Were Born* describes to the newborn the wondrous processes of nature that were occurring on that day. Mem Fox's informal letter in book format, *Whoever You Are*, celebrates the fact that, whoever you are, you share feelings and humanity with other children all over the world. And in a more humorous vein, Jamie Lee Curtis' *Tell Me Again About the Night I Was Born* has the feeling of a family album in which a child is recounting the birth memories her parents have lovingly sent to her.

Other types of informal correspondence can be modeled through sharing of your own cards and notes or through children's books that use a letter-writing format. We have included here examples of books, both realistic and fantastical, that feature letters to family and friends, and letters for particular purposes, such as invitations or postcards sent while traveling.

Informal Correspondence

Birth Letters

Casely, J. 1991. *Dear Annie*. New York: Greenwillow. (P)
> See text.

Curtis, J.L. 1997. *Tell Me Again About the Night I Was Born*. New York: HarperCollins. (P)
> See text.

Fox, M. 1997. *Whoever You Are*. Illus. by L. Staub. San Diego: Harcourt Brace. (P)
> See text.

Frazier, D. 1991. *On the Day You Were Born*. San Diego: Harcourt Brace. (P)
> See text.

Letters to Family and Friends

Anholt, L. 1996. *The Magpie Song*. Boston: Houghton Mifflin. (P)
> Carla and her grandfather exchange letters describing their very difficult lives in the city and the country.

Asch, F. 1992. *Dear Brother*. New York: Scholastic. (P)

Two boys read a collection of old family letters they find in the attic of their house.

Danziger, P. & A.M. Martin. 1998. *P.S. Longer Letter Later*. New York: Scholastic. (U)

Two friends, separated when one moves away, share long letters that discuss their difficulties with family problems and friendships.

DuPasquier, P. 1985. *Dear Daddy*. New York: Bradbury. (P)

Sophie writes letters to her seaman father over the course of a year, and the illustrations show both her activities and what her father does as he works and travels.

Rodell, S. 1995. *Dear Fred*. Illus. by K. Gimble. New York: Ticknor and Fields. (P)

A girl writes to her brother to say how much she misses him when her family is separated by divorce.

Selway, M. 1994. *I Hate Roland Roberts*. Nashville, TN: Ideals. (P)

In letters to her grandfather, a girl describes her new school and the boy who teases her.

Spurr, E. 1996. *The Long, Long Letter*. Illus. by D. Catrow. New York: Hyperion. (P)

A woman writes a long, long letter to her sister, with surprising results, in this tall tale about letter writing.

Letters for a Special Purpose

Ada, A.F. 1994. *Dear Peter Rabbit*. Illus. by L. Tryon. New York: Simon & Schuster. (U/P)

A series of letters between fairy tale characters culminates in an invitation to a party.

———. 1998. *Yours Truly, Goldilocks*. Illus. by L. Tryon. New York: Aladdin. (U/P)

This sequel is a continuation of the correspondence begun in *Dear Peter Rabbit*, after the party is over.

Ahlberg, J. & A. Ahlberg. 1986. *The Jolly Postman Or Other People's Letters*. Boston: Little, Brown. (U/P)

An earlier set of correspondence among fairy tale characters.

———. 1995. *The Jolly Pocket Postman*. Boston: Little, Brown. (U/P)

Letters, postcards, fliers, and booklets of many sorts are delivered to fairy tale characters by the Jolly Postman.

Bat-Ami, M. 1995. *Dear Elijah*. New York: Farrar, Straus & Giroux. (U)

Because her father is ill, Rebecca begins to question her Jewish faith, so she writes a series of letters to the prophet Elijah, in which she shares her struggles.

Bedard, M. 1992. *Emily*. Illus. by B. Cooney. New York: Doubleday. (U/P)

This book contains a fictional letter from Emily Dickinson.

Brisson, P. 1989. *Your Best Friend, Kate*. New York: Bradbury. (P)

Kate uses notes to tell her best friend good-bye, as well as to communicate with her brother.

———. 1990. *Kate Heads West*. New York: Bradbury. (P)

While on a vacation to the west, Kate writes letters home.

———. 1992. *Kate on the Coast*. New York: Bradbury. (P)

Kate sends letters to friends back home as she travels on vacation.

Harrison, J. 1994. *Dear Bear*. Minneapolis: CarolRhoda Books. (P)

Katie fears the bear that lives under the stairs, until they begin to exchange letters.

Leedy, L. 1993. *Postcards from Pluto: A Tour of the Solar System*. New York: Holiday. (U/P)

A series of hand-written postcards is delivered from an imaginary class of students touring the solar system.

Livingston, M.C. 1989. "Invitation." In *Birthday Poems*. New York: Holiday. (P)

A birthday invitation in rhyme is included in this collection.

Samton, S. 1991. *Jenny's Journey*. New York: Viking. (P)

When Jenny's friend, Maria, who has moved away, writes to say she is lonely, Jenny writes a long, imaginative letter describing how she will travel to see her.

Spedden, D.C. 1994. *Polar, the Titanic Bear*. Toronto: Madison Press. (P)

Letters, photographs, and postcards from an actual stuffed bear who survived the wreck of the Titanic along with his young owner.

Swanson, S.M. 1998. *Letter to the Lake*. Illus. by P. Catalanotto. New York: DK. (P)

As she experiences the cold of winter, Rosie writes a letter, full of warm memories, to the lake where she spent the summer.

Willard, N. 1997. *The Magic Cornfield*. San Diego: Harcourt Brace. (U)

Postcards from a character trapped in a magic corn field display all of the conventions of good writing but within a fantastic context.

Williams, V.B. & J. Williams. 1988. *Stringbean's Trip to the Shining Sea*. New York: Greenwillow. (P)

Stringbean sends a series of postcards from places he visits on a cross-country trip to friends and family.

Yolen, J. 1992. *A Letter from Phoenix Farm*. Katonah, NY: Richard C. Owen. (U)

Yolen writes, in letter form, her autobiography for children.

_____. 1995. "Letter to the Moon." In *Blast Off!*, ed. L.B. Hopkins. New York: HarperCollins. (P)

This is a letter in the form of a poem, written to the moon to apologize for human intrusion.

Special-Occasion Correspondence: Valentines

Valentines may be the type of correspondence with which children are most familiar. Valentine's Day can be a wonderful experience for children, but also one of dark despair when valentines are hurtful or expected but not received. Older elementary students often engage in terrible teasing of one another based on the quality and quantity of valentines received from others in class. Teachers can turn this day into a special time for thinking about the impact of letters by sharing books in which valentines play a special role. They might share Robert Sabuda's brief biography of St. Valentine, which suggests that the first valentine was a letter of friendship between a young blind girl and the later martyred Valentine, who was her teacher. The valentine was a token of friendship rather than a token of romance.

Sending and Receiving Valentines

Barkin, C. & E. James. 1988. *Happy Valentine's Day*. Illus. by M. Weston. New York: Lothrop. (U/P)

This book includes the history of the holiday as well as recipes and valentine-making suggestions.

Graham-Barber, L. 1991. *The Complete Book of Valentine Words*. Illus. by B. Lewin. New York: Bradbury. (U)

Origins and history of terms, from *chocolate* to *sweetheart*, are discussed.

Hoban, L. 1998. *Silly Tilly's Valentine*. New York: HarperCollins. (P)

Tilly, a mole, almost forgets to remember it's Valentine's Day in this *I Can Read* story.

Hopkins, L.B. 1976. *Good Morning to You, Valentine*. Illus. by T. De Paola. San Diego: Harcourt Brace. (U/P)

This volume of twenty-three poems includes poems on giving and receiving valentines.

Sabuda, R. 1992. *Saint Valentine*. New York: Simon & Schuster. (U)

See text.

Shannon, G. 1995. *Heart to Heart*. Illus. by Steve Bjorkman. Boston: Houghton Mifflin. (P)

Squirrel makes his friend Mole a one-of-a-kind valentine full of things that help them remember happy times they have had together.

Sharmat, M.W. 1994. *Nate the Great and the Mushy Valentine*. Illus. by M. Simont. New York: Delacorte. (P)

Nate solves two strange cases involving a missing valentine and a mysterious one.

Stamper, J.B. 1993. *Valentine Holiday Grab Bag*. Illus. by B. Weissman & T.R. Garcia. New Jersey: Troll. (U/P)

This history of the holiday includes ideas for activities and valentines to make.

Stevenson, J. 1995. A *Village Full of Valentines*. New York: Greenwillow. (P)

Each animal in a village celebrates Valentine's Day in a unique way.

Twohill, M. 1991. *Valentine Frankenstein*. New York: Bradbury. (U)

Amanda stuffs the Valentine's Day box in her classroom so that her friend, Walter, will feel popular, but her plan backfires.

Other Special-Occasion Correspondence

All holidays offer occasions for writing. Celebrations of any type feature treasured recipes of favorite foods, invitations to particular events, letters and cards expressing our feelings for others, and, of course, thank-you notes for gifts received. Holiday correspondence provides a once- or twice-a-year connection with people who are on our minds, but not a part of our daily lives. Sending and receiving holiday mail is a tradition in many families.

For most of our students, their own birthday is an occasion for writing, including party invitations, lists of people to invite, things to do, and good things to eat. Children's books model the politenesses of birthday etiquette and can be used for literary occasions in classrooms. One second-grade classroom celebrated the birthday of their favorite author, Dr. Seuss, sending invitations to parents, the school librarian, and other adults that were fans of his. They planned a menu of Dr. Seuss refreshments, including green eggs and ham and roast beast, and printed their menu for each guest. During the party they dramatized their favorite scenes from Dr. Seuss books, and after it was over, they sent thank-you notes to the people who helped them find books and make refreshments. Another classroom, taking their cues from Janet and Allan Ahlbergs' *The Jolly Postman* and Alma Flor Ada's *Dear Peter*

Rabbit and *Yours Truly, Goldilocks*, planned a birthday party for their favorite fairy tale characters, creating invitations and party correspondence similar to those included in these books.

Christmas is perhaps the American holiday that is most celebrated through writing and is most modeled in children's literature. Children make gift lists to Santa, write part or all of the family Christmas letter, and thank family and friends for gifts received. Not all of our students celebrate Christmas. Many schools have moved to Winter festivals in lieu of Christmas, and Fall or Harvest Festivals in lieu of Halloween, celebrating the fact that people have honored the changes of the seasons even as they also honor particular religious and patriotic occasions. We might encourage students to write seasonally, sharing stories, traditions, correspondence, and other forms of writing appropriate to occasions.

Again, children's books can provide models for these writings. In Bruce Koscielniak's *Geoffrey Groundhog Predicts the Weather*, a celebration of our annual hopes for an early spring, Geoffrey's progress is tracked through a series of newspaper stories that follow the events. Joan Anderson's*The Glorious Fourth at Prairietown*, a reconstruction of an 1836 Fourth of July celebration, includes entries from the log of a young boy, Joshua, who is a participant. Jean Craighead George's *Dear Rebecca, Winter is Here* celebrates the changes of the season in a letter written by a grandmother to her granddaughter on December 21, the shortest day of the year.

Other Special-Occasion Correspondence

Birthdays

Ada, A.F. 1994. *Dear Peter Rabbit*. Illus. by L. Tryon. New York: Atheneum. (P)
   See text.
_____. 1998. *Yours Truly, Goldilocks*. Illus. by L. Tryon. New York:
   Atheneum. (P)
   See text.
Ahlberg, J. & A. Ahlberg. 1986. The *Jolly Postman or Other People's Letters*.
   Boston: Little, Brown. (P)
   See text.

Christmas

Ahlberg, J. & A. Ahlberg. 1991. The *Jolly Christmas Postman*. Boston:
   Little, Brown. (P)

Christmas letters and small gifts from fairy tale characters are included in this book.

Hausman, S. 1972. *Yes, Virginia*. New York: Elizabeth Press. (P)
The story of the letter written by a little girl to the editor of a New York newspaper, asking if there is a Santa Claus and his famous reply.

Tolkien, J.R.R. 1991.*The Father Christmas Letters*. Boston: Houghton Mifflin. (U/P)
Tolkien created these letters and sent them to his own children, as if he were Father Christmas.

Wild, M. 1992. *Thank You, Santa*. Illus. by K. Argent. New York: Scholastic. (P)
A little girl becomes Santa's pen pal, and he shares information with her about the animals that live at the North Pole.

Seasons

Anderson, J. 1986. *The Glorious Fourth at Prairietown*. Illus. by G. Ancona. New York: Morrow. (U)
See text.

George, J.C. 1993. *Dear Rebecca, Winter Is Here*. Illus. by L. Kupinski. New York: HarperCollins. (P)
See text.

Koscielniak, B. 1995. *Geoffrey Groundhog Predicts the Weather*. Boston: Houghton Mifflin. (P)
See text.

Pen Pals

The best kinds of letters to receive may well be the unsolicited ones, the ones that tell not only something about the sender, but also something about yourself and your place in the world. These types of letters appear in books for children as well. In Betsy Byars' *Cracker Jackson*, Cracker receives an unsolicited letter from his former babysitter, whom he has helped to rescue from an abusive relationship. The letter conveys her love for him and reflects a growing understanding of herself and Cracker's place in her life. Similarly, in Patricia Reilly Giff's *The War Began at Supper: Letters to Miss Loria*, several students correspond with a former student teacher. During the course of exchanging letters, the students share their concerns about school, friendships, and the Persian Gulf Crisis. Through exchanging letters, the children gain insight into themselves, their classmates, and the war, in which a classmate's father is fighting. The children have an opportunity to reflect on what they want to communicate to others, as well as what they expect back from them.

Electronic mail has expanded our uses of correspondence in many schools and classrooms. Programs that encourage electronic pen pals in other classes, schools, cities, or countries allow children to write their thoughts, ideas, and questions about others and get relatively speedy replies. The instant gratification of electronic pen pals means that children can see right away the satisfactions of two-way communication. On the other hand, the slow sweetness of sending a letter by "snail mail," as electronic users call postal service correspondence, provides a different kind of satisfaction. The anticipation of the receiver's delight in opening the letter, the time to be thoughtful before sending a reply, and the chance to reread the favorite parts are advantages of the slower process. Arnold Lobel used "snail mail," long before the term was invented for e-mail users, in his Frog and Toad story, "The Letter." In this simple story, Frog writes a letter to his friend Toad, who feels very sorry for himself. Because the letter is delivered by a snail, Toad has several days to consider his sadness, and Frog has several days of delighted anticipation of his gift of a letter before it arrives to cheer up Toad.

Pen Pals

Bonners, S. 1997. *The Silver Balloon*. New York: Farrar, Straus & Giroux. (U)
Gregory, a lonely fourth-grader, ties a card with his name and address to a helium balloon, which leads to correspondence with a special older pen pal.

Broome, E. 1994. *Dear Mr. Sprouts*. New York: Random House. (U)
A boy writes letters from the Australian bush to a secretive pen pal.

Byars, B. 1986. *Cracker Jackson*. New York: Puffin. (U)
See text.

Giff, P.R. 1991. *The War Began at Supper: Letters to Miss Loria*. New York: Delacorte. (U)
See text.

Lobel, A. 1970. *Frog and Toad Are Friends*. New York: HarperCollins. (P)
See text.

Lorbiecki, M. 1997. My *Palace of Leaves in Sarajevo*. New York: Dial. (U)
A set of fictional letters between two cousins, one who is surviving the

war in the former Yugoslavia, and the other who is trying to offer her hope from her home in Minnesota.

Wilson, B. 1992. "The Pen Pal." In *The Leaving.* New York: Philomel. (U)

At the end of this short story, a girl discovers that her Australian pen pal, to whom she has bared her soul, is not a girl but a boy.

Formal Correspondence

A second category of correspondence, formal correspondence, requires children to converse with people with whom they don't necessarily share their lives. Correspondents may include a favorite author, a research librarian, an expert in a particular field, or an advice columnist in a newspaper or magazine. When children conduct formal correspondence, it is important that they be sincere. Beverly Cleary's novel *Dear Mr. Henshaw* describes how a contrived school assignment of writing a letter to a favorite author became meaningful when the content of the letters and the feelings of the correspondents were authentic instead of forced.

In the novel, Leigh Botts is required to write to an author and to include a list of questions generated by his teacher about the writer's life and his writing habits. Mr. Henshaw, the author, is clearly fed up with spending his writing time doing homework assignments for students. He writes back that he won't answer Leigh's questions until Leigh tells him similar things about himself. Although Leigh is offended, his mother insists he answer Mr. Henshaw honestly. Here begins a genuine correspondence between author and reader, one in which Leigh is willing to share more about himself with a correspondent who comes to mean a great deal to him.

It may be necessary to model formal and informal correspondence in order for students to see the similarities and the differences. Sometimes young writers aren't sure of the right tone to take in their letters. Sharing samples, both fictional and actual, can be part of a minilesson on purpose and audience, two factors that influence letter writing. The book *Sincerely Yours: How to Write Great Letters*, by Elizabeth James and Carol Barkin, provides practical tips for making correspondence simple. The authors explain how to write thank-you notes, apologies, invitations, and family letters, and they show examples of each written by children. The book also contains samples of formal correspondence, ranging from letters of request to letters that may be published in an advice column.

It is important to remember that initial letters to any sender may look different from those exchanged over time. As relationships evolve through writing, the language used by the sender and the receiver is likely to become less formal. Teachers may want to read Helene Hanff's *84 Charing Cross Road*, a set of letters between the author and two booksellers in London during World War II, to remind themselves of this process of growth. The early letters in this long correspondence are brief and businesslike. As the war goes on, the writers learn more about each other and wartime troubles. By the end of the book, a powerful friendship is portrayed in the letters.

Beginning in the first grade, most language arts textbooks contain chapters on how to write a letter. Often, the writing assignments resemble Leigh Botts' original letter to Mr. Henshaw. However, with all the authentic opportunities that exist for students to do formal and informal correspondence, it seems unnecessary for them to practice letter writing with contrived activities. Acknowledging the kinds of correspondence that need to be conducted, and using class time to conduct, it seems like a more relevant approach. When children are writing letters to transact business or to sustain personal relationships, they are motivated to complete tasks in "proper" ways. It is in this context that the parts of the letter (heading; inside address, if appropriate; greeting; body; closing; and signature) and the proper ways to address an envelope (return address and recipient's address) can be presented most successfully.

Formal Correspondence

Avi. 1991. *Nothing but the Truth*. New York: Orchard. (U)
  This "documentary" novel uses both formal and informal correspondence, including letters, memos, and diary entries, to question authorities and defend one's position.
Bunin, S. 1995. *Dear Great American Writers School*. Boston: Houghton Mifflin. (U)
  A young girl writes a series of letters to a mail order writing school, where an employee, moved by her enthusiasm, tries to encourage her.
Cleary, B. 1983. *Dear Mr. Henshaw*. New York: Dell. (U)
  See text.
Colbert, J. & A. Harms. 1998. *Dear Doctor King: Letters from Today's Children to Dr. Martin Luther King, Jr.* New York: Hyperion. (U/P)

Like those in her previous book, *Anni's India Diary*, the brief passages in this fictional work describe Anni's travel adventures.

Byars, B. 1989. *Bingo Brown and the Language of Love*. New York: Viking. (U)
See text.

———. 1990. *The Burning Questions of Bingo Brown*. New York: Puffin. (U)
See text.

Casely, J. 1997. *Jorah's Journal*. New York: Greenwillow. (P)
Jorah's move, her new school, friendships, and a birthday are recorded in her journal, hand-printed on the pages of this fictional book.

Cleary, B. 1991. *Strider*. New York: Morrow. (U)
Leigh Botts survived through his journal in *Dear Mr. Henshaw* and continues it in this sequel.

George, J.C. 1989. *My Side of the Mountain*. New York: Dutton. (U)
Sam keeps a journal of his summer alone in the wilderness.

Hesse, K. 1996. *The Music of Dolphins*. New York: Scholastic. (U)
A feral child learns to speak and write English, and her reactions to being "civilized" are recorded in this journal.

Hest, A. 1995. *The Private Notebook of Katie Roberts, Age 11*. Illus. by S. Lamut. Cambridge, MA: Candlewick. (U)
This book contains fictional journal entries by Katie, whose mother remarries after her father is killed in World War II and who moves with her new family to Texas.

Hirsch, K. 1994. *Ellen Anders on Her Own*. New York: Simon & Schuster. (U)
After Ellen's mother dies, she finds her mother's seventh-grade diary, which comforts Ellen and helps her with problems she is having in school.

Kalman, E. 1994. *Tchaikovsky Discovers America*. New York: Orchard. (U)
Tchaikovsky's observations during his trip to America in 1891 are interwoven with the fictional diary of an 11-year-old girl.

Lobel, A. 1979. *Frog and Toad Together*. New York: HarperCollins. (P)
See text.

Lowry, L. 1979. *Anastasia Krupnik*. Boston: Houghton Mifflin.
See text.

Moss, M. 1995. *Amelia's Notebook*. Berkeley, CA: Tricycle Press.

———. 1996. *Amelia Writes Again*. Berkeley, CA: Tricycle Press.

———. 1998. *Amelia Hits the Road*. Berkeley, CA: Tricycle Press. (All U/P)
Amelia chronicles her days through the year and summer vacations in these diaries with pictures and humorous asides.

Sharmat, M.W. 1997. *Richie and the Fritzes*. New York: HarperCollins. (P)
In this volume for early readers, alternating journal entries tell Richie and Annie's versions of a lost-dog incident.

Snyder, Z.K. 1990. *Libby on Wednesday*. New York: Delacorte. (U)

   Libby keeps a journal for use in her writing group.

Yolen, J. 1979. *The Giants Go Camping*. New York: Clarion. (P)

   See text.

Some of the letters we send to ourselves are disposable. We write them, read them, and then destroy them. They are letters in which we try out writing about our feelings; once they are written, we no longer need to send them. Because students may do some of their self-correspondence in school, privacy is essential. Teachers may want to create a Dead Letter Box, which is sealed, and invite children to deposit self-correspondence within.

Other letters, we keep. We use them to record our hopes and fears. In addition, the format of a letter lets us talk to someone who may not be available and to use the talk to anchor our lives. For example, in Karen Hesse's *Letters from Rifka*, Rifka writes letters to her cousin in Russia throughout her escape to America. She knows the letters can never reach Tovah, but admits that she feels less frightened by writing them. Similarly, Harriet Ann talks to her mama, who has passed away, in *Letters from a Slave Girl*, in an effort to ease her loneliness. We can help our students to see that the act of writing letters is important; mailing them may not be.

If you've never experimented with letters as a form of self-talk or kept a journal or a diary, you might enjoy reading Carla Stevens' *A Book of Your Own: Keeping a Diary or a Journal*, written for children but appropriate for all writers. Stevens discusses what to put in a diary or a journal, how to keep a diary or a journal private, and ways to use it to organize the activities of daily life. She also explains how diaries and journals helped writers, such as E.B. White, create their best-loved books (70).

Historical Correspondence

Children who are writing diaries, journals, and letters may also want to read actual and fictional correspondence written by others. Such correspondence may comprise entire books or be clustered around a particular subject. For example, children who are studying an historical event in social studies, such as the Westward Movement, can research journals, diaries, and actual letters written during the 1800s as well as read fictional accounts. Both genres capture the trek along the Oregon, California, and Mormon Trails in first person. Correspondence surrounding the long journey provides children with a perspective that cannot be gleaned from informational books alone.

Fictional books that use the letter-writing format and focus on particular events in history draw on actual accounts. This is evident in the collection of letters exchanged between ten-year-old Nadja and her cousin Alex, which is entitled *My Palace of Leaves in Sarajevo*. The author, Marybeth Lorbiecki, writes, "When the war erupted, Sarajevans had to decide if they wanted to leave, fight their neighbors, or work to save friendships and hope for peace. The things Nadja writes of are true" (Lorbiecki 1997, Introduction).

Historical correspondence emanates from family stories, personal interviews, and memory, as well as from research. It captures the urgency of life through reflection and recall. As a genre, historical correspondence offers much to students. The titles listed here include books written in epistolary style (letters), as well as narratives evoked from journal entries. The journals and diaries make history real; they provide personal perspectives, fictionalized or actual, of important events, and they have the potential to hook children on reading and keeping written records of their own.

Historical Correspondence

Letters

Hesse, K. 1992. *Letters from Rifka*. New York: Holt. (U)
    See text.
Lorbiecki, M. 1997. *My Palace of Leaves in Sarajevo*. New York: Dial. (U)
    See text.
Lyons, M.E. 1992. *Letters from a Slave Girl: The Story of Harriet Jacobs*.
    New York: Simon & Schuster. (U)
    See text.
Nichol, B. 1993. *Beethoven Lives Upstairs*. Illus. by S. Cameron. New York:
    Orchard. (U/P)
    When Beethoven, who is going deaf, rents a room in his mother's house,
    a young boy records his reactions to the difficult genius.
Pinkney, A.D. 1994. *Dear Benjamin Banneker*. Illus. by B. Pinkney.
    New York: Gulliver. (U/P)
    This brief biography of Bannecker, a self-taught African-American in-
    ventor, describes a letter he sent to Thomas Jefferson, questioning
    Jefferson's position on slavery.

Uchida, Y. 1990. "Letter from a Concentration Camp." In *The Big Book for Peace*, ed. A. Durrell & M. Sachs. New York: Dutton. (U)

A young boy sends a letter to a friend, describing conditions at Tanforan Internment Camp.

Woodruff, E. 1994. *Dear Levi: Letters from the Overland Trail*. New York: Knopf. (U)

Twelve-year-old Austin writes these letters to his brother as his family travels the Oregon Trail.

Diaries and Journals

Besson, J.L. 1995. *October 45: Childhood Memories of the War*. Mankato, MN: Creative Editions. (U)

A memoir of wartime France, with cartoon drawings, this reads like a diary or journal.

Brighton, C. 1997. *My Napoleon*. Brookfield, CT: Millbrook Press. (U)

A fictional journal based on events in the life of an English girl whose father took in Napoleon as a guest after his defeat at Waterloo.

Columbus, C. 1990. *I, Columbus: My Journal*. Illus. by P.E. Hanson. New York: Walker. (U)

Entries extracted from Columbus' journal describe his voyage to the Americas.

_____. 1992. *The Log of Christopher Columbus: The First Voyage, Spring, Summer, and Fall 1492*. Illus. by R. Sabuda. New York: Philomel. (P)

For younger readers, a brief illustrated set of entries from Columbus' log.

Dear America Series. New York: Scholastic. (U)

For this series of readable books, respected authors of historical fiction for children have created fictional diaries and journals of girls who might have lived through historic events in the American past.

Donahue, J. 1994. *An Island Far from Home*. Minneapolis: CarolRhoda. (U)

Twelve-year-old Joshua exchanges letters with a fourteen-year-old Confederate prisoner at the insistence of his family, and both writers must reconsider who is the enemy.

Duey, K. *American Diaries* Series. New York: Simon & Schuster. (U)

Currently, there are eleven volumes in this series of diaries of girls who lived during significant times in American history.

Hopkinson, D. 1997. *Birdie's Lighthouse*. Illus. by K. Root. New York: Atheneum. (U/P)

Based on the experiences of several women lighthouse keepers of the nineteenth century, this picture book shares diary entries written by a young woman named Birdie.

Krupinski, L. 1995. *Bluewater Journal: The Voyage of the Sea Tiger*. New York: HarperCollins. (U/P)

A boy traveling with his family around the Cape to California keeps a journal of the trip.

Lyons, M.E. 1995. *Keeping Secrets: The Girlhood Diaries of Seven Women Writers*. New York: Holt. (U)

The diaries of seven writers, including Louisa May Alcott and Charlotte Perkins Gilman, are described and excerpted.

Macaulay, D. 1983. *Mill*. Boston: Houghton Mifflin. (U)

The history of a fictional New England mill is told through drawings, diary entries, and text.

———. 1993. *Ship*. Boston: Houghton Mifflin. (U)

The plans for, building, and voyages of a clipper ship are detailed in this volume with a fictional storyline.

Moss, M. 1998. *Rachel's Journal: The Story of a Pioneer Girl*. San Diego: Harcourt Brace. (U/P)

Handwritten and embellished with notes and drawings, these journal entries describe Rachel and her family's trip overland to California by covered wagon in 1850.

My Name Is America Series. New York: Scholastic.

This companion series to the Dear America series features boys who lived through historic events.

Rabin, S. 1994. *Casey Over There*. San Diego: Harcourt Brace. (P)

When Aubrey's brother, who has been writing to him from France during World War I, stops writing, Aubrey writes a letter to Uncle Sam.

Roop, P. & C. Roop, eds. 1993. *Off the Map: The Journals of Lewis and Clark*. Illus. by B. Tanner. New York: Walker. (U)

Entries from the journals of Lewis and Clark give readers a sense of the discoveries these explorers made in the American West.

Shuter, J., ed. 1996. *Sarah Royce and the American West*. Austin: Raintree. (U)

Based on Royce's diary of her journey to California by covered wagon, this illustrated version also contains sidebars with background information to clarify her observations.

Tunnell, M.O. & G.W. Chilcoat. 1996. *The Children of Topaz: The Story of a Japanese-American Internment Camp*. New York: Holiday. (U)

Based on a teacher's journal kept at the internment camp, this nonfiction book follows the lives of the children who were interned there.

Turner, A. 1997. *Mississippi Mud: Three Prairie Journals*. Illus. by J. Blake. New York: HarperCollins. (U/P)

This is a book of journal entries in the form of poems written by three young people traveling to Oregon with their family by covered wagon.

Delivering the Mail

Although we may complain about the post office, many of us have a real affection for our local post office and our mail carrier. We feel connected to this person who knows our dog's name, who greets us cheerily each day, bringing news of family and friends and the latest wish books and catalogues. The Ahlbergs have captured this person in their Jolly Postman Series, a bicycling fellow who stops for tea and brings the news, both good and bad, from out in the world. Uri Shulevitz' *Toddlecreek Post Office* and Kevin Henkes' *Good-Bye Curtis* are testaments to the small local post office and mail carrier who has been a friend.

The history of our mail service is a fascinating one. The romance of delivering the mail is best represented in the books available on the young men who rode for the Pony Express. Sometimes the stories are strange. Michael Tunnel's *Mailing May* tells of an actual incident when a child was mailed because riding in the mail car of the train was cheaper than riding as a passenger. Some of us have collected stamps and have seen how they have changed over time and place. Students who are writing letters might want to spend time thinking about the people who, like Lobel's snail, deliver the mail. They might want to send a thank-you letter to their mail carrier or study the people who have delivered the mail.

■■■

Delivering the Mail

Ahlberg, J. & A. Ahlberg. 1986. *The Jolly Postman*. Boston: Little, Brown. (U/P)

———. 1995. *The Jolly Pocket Postman*. Boston: Little, Brown. (U/P)
A fictional postman delivers letters by bicycle to various fairy tale characters in these two volumes.

Glass, A. 1995. *The Sweetwater Run: The Story of Buffalo Bill Cody and the Pony Express*. New York: Doubleday. (P)
A picture book explores Cody's experiences when, as a boy, he rode for the Pony Express across Wyoming.

Gregory, K. 1994. *Jimmy Spoon and the Pony Express*. New York: Scholastic. (U)
A sequel to *The Legend of Jimmy Spoon*, this novel describes Jimmy's interest in becoming a rider for the Pony Express.

Harness, C. 1996. *They're Off! The Story of the Pony Express*. New York: Simon & Schuster. (U/P)
Watercolor paintings and detailed maps enhance this picture book history.

Henkes, K. 1995. *Good-Bye Curtis*. New York: Greenwillow. (P)

Chapter Four

Who's Counting?
Using Writing and Literature to Understand Mathematics

Introduction

While we generally think of math and literacy as different subjects, reading, writing, listening, and discussion are tools children can use as they strive to understand and communicate the language of mathematics. Teachers can introduce any math concept with a writing or a drawing. Ask children to tell you in a personal letter what they know, think, and feel about the topic. Encourage them to write freely, honestly, and thoughtfully. Sometimes a provocative question can be an impetus to writing: What is a number? Have you ever heard of the word *subtraction*? What do you think about or feel when you hear the word *million*? Young children may want to begin their thinking by using a drawing or dictating their ideas to a scribe. The writing or artwork will reveal what children already know about the concept, the failures or successes they may have experienced, and provide the information needed to implement the study. Another way to determine what children bring to the concept is to do a group jot list or web, or compile information from their individual writings. After the teacher understands what her students know, she can collect books, manipulative materials, and charts to create displays that feature the concept. Children might begin by sharing already published books and then constructing their own. Primary students may work together to construct a counting big book or a big book about a number. After a comment by a first-grader on the number of threes featured in folk tales, such as three pigs, three bears, and three billy goats gruff, a group of children made a big book of threes, adding pages for these and three blind mice, three little kittens, and the three balls Cinderella attended.

Math Attitudes

Children may have strong opinions about math, some developing out of their own failures to grasp the abstract principles of mathematics, and others coming from some of the tedium of doing many sheets of problems or story problems. Jon Scieszka's hilarious *Math Curse*, a picture book illustrated by Lane Smith, shows the mind-boggling troubles a child encounters once her teacher tells her, "You know, you can think of almost everything you do as a math problem." The student realizes that from the moment she tries to figure out what shirt to wear to school, through geography lessons involving distances, through lunch with fractions of pizza and apple pie, all the way to bedtime and the decision as to what time to wake up in the morning, she is doing math. By the end of the story, she admits, all this math is *no problem* and the math curse is broken, but she is challenged again when her teacher says, "You know, you can think of almost everything as a science experiment."

Poetry also provides a number of examples of attitudes toward mathematics that can give children models for their own thinking and writing. Mathematics and poetry seem to come from opposite sides of the spectrum: Mathematics is about numbers and rules of operation; poetry is about language and feelings. Yet mathematics and poetry are alike in many ways. Both are language processes; both involve an orderly presentation of abstracts; both try to get to the root understandings of things around us.

Two of children's favorite poems about math troubles appear in Kalli Dakos' *If You're Not Here, Please Raise Your Hand*, which will appeal to middle-level students. Her "Math is Brewing and I'm in Trouble" suggests making a witches brew of numbers and saving the world from "brains all stretched and gnarled and fried, with countless numbers multiplied." Dakos' "They Don't Do Math in Texas" speaks of a student's envy when the new girl in school tells her class about this.

Dakos' poetry collection for younger children, *Mrs. Cole on an Onion Roll and Other School Poems*, includes a four-line poem about getting all the answers to arithmetic problems wrong and, as a result, making the day very long. Similarly, George Ulrich's *The Spook Matinee and Other Scary Poems for Kids* includes "Tigers Don't Scare Me," a poem about the true meaning of fear: being quizzed on math problems. Children might want to write about their fears of getting the wrong answer or other math fears, using these poems as models. The poems children write will give teachers good clues about their attitudes and struggles with math. Teachers might write their own poems, with memories of the difficulties of math and math tests, so that their students can see that many of us have struggled and we can work together to make math less frightening.

Several poets have parodied the forms and structures of mathematics they learned in elementary school. Story problems, for example, can be frustrating because they deal with experiences children often have not had, like train scheduling times. Arnold Adoff's *Chocolate Dreams* includes two story problem poems. "The Old Math. One" starts with the classic description of two trains leaving their stations at given times and speeds, but the trains, carrying chocolate, collide in a Colorado town, causing a chocolate disaster. "The Old Math. Two" puts together blocks of chocolate and times of day plus one chocolate eater, ending in the line, "I love to subtract." Carl Sandburg's "Arithmetic" is popular with children because it mocks the story problem with silly situations such as, if you eat the two eggs your mother has fried for you when you only asked for one, "who is better at arithmetic, you or your mother?" Students who are creating their own story problems might also like to write a poem that humorously looks at "The Old Math," as Adoff calls it, creating a silly story problem about a favorite thing or event.

Mathematics doesn't have to be frightening or boring. In any classroom you will also find students who love mathematics. Poets, too, have celebrated the beauty of numbers, of math functions, and even of the instruments we use in solving problems. Georgia Heard's "Compass" is an instrument she describes as creating circles of "mathematical perfection." Students might want to write a poem to celebrate the ruler, a calculator, an abacus, or another mathematical device. Eve Merriam is another poet who celebrates mathematics. After reading such poems of Merriam's as "Zero" and "Gazinta," students might want to write their own poems in praise of a favorite number or concept. Barbara wrote the following poem as she thought about all of the terms we use for addition:

I am the Count of Numbers.
I shout out "Tally ho!"
The total of my followers
just seems to grow and grow.
My subjects I can't calculate;
they increase as they come.
Oh who can help me figure out
the answer to this sum?

Books and Poems with Math Attitudes

Adoff, A. 1989a. "The Old Math. One." In *Chocolate Dreams*. Illus. by
T. MacCombie. New York: Lothrop. (U)

_____. 1989b. "The Old Math. Two." In *Chocolate Dreams*. Illus. by
T. MacCombie. New York: Lothrop. (U)
See text.

Dakos, K. 1990a. "Math Is Brewing and I'm in Trouble." In *If You're Not
Here, Please Raise Your Hand: Poems About School*. Illus. by G.B. Karas.
New York: Macmillan. (U/P)

_____. 1990b. "They Don't Do Math in Texas." In *If You're Not Here,
Please Raise Your Hand: Poems About School*. Illus. by G.B. Karas.
New York: Macmillan. (U/P)

_____. 1990c. "The Wind Is Calling Me Away." In *If You're Not Here,
Please Raise Your Hand: Poems About School*. Illus. by G.B. Karas. New
York: Macmillan. (U/P)
See text.

_____. 1995. "This Day Is Going to Be Very Loooooooooooooooong." In
Mrs. Cole on an Onion Roll and Other School Poems. Illus. by J. Adinolfi.
New York: Simon & Schuster. (P)
See text.

Heard, G. 1996. "Compass." In *School Supplies: A Book of Poems*, ed.
L.B. Hopkins. Illus. by R. Flower. New York: Simon & Schuster. (U)
See text.

Merriam, E. 1987. "Zero." In *Halloween ABC*. Illus. by L. Smith. New York:
Macmillan. (U)
See text.

_____. 1989. "Gazinta." In *Chortles*. Illus. by S. Hamanaka. New York:
Morrow. (U)
See text.

Sandburg, C. 1982. "Arithmetic." In *Rainbows Are Made*, ed. L.B. Hopkins. San Diego: Harcourt Brace. (U)
   See text.

Scieszka, J. 1995. *Math Curse*. Illus. by L. Smith. New York: Viking. (U/P)
   See text.

Ulrich, G. 1992. "Tigers Don't Scare Me." In *The Spook Matinee and Other Scary Poems for Kids*. New York: Delacorte. (P)
   See text.

A Unit on Counting

Primary-grade units on counting and numbers provide rich opportunities for mathematical language experiences. Children might start by recalling some of the nursery rhymes and songs they know that include numbers. They might come up with "Baa Baa Black Sheep" or "One, Two, Buckle My Shoe" for nursery rhymes and "This Old Man" and "Ten in a Bed" for songs. Children who come from other language backgrounds might recite "Un elefante" in Spanish or "Eins, zwei, polizei" in German, helping their classmates to understand that counting rhymes have been shared with children in many cultures and languages. After pooling their previous knowledge, students can explore books of nursery rhymes and songs for other rhymes that include numbers. They might create books or large charts with their own versions of traditional chants and songs. In one such song, a group of children featured their own classroom: "There were ten in a desk and the little one said, "Move over, move over . . .""

Counting Songs and Chants

Individual Counting Songs and Nursery Rhyme Chants (All P)

Ahlberg, A. 1991. *Ten in a Bed*. New York: Puffin.

O'Donnell, E. 1991. *The Twelve Days of Summer*. Illus. by K.L. Schmidt. New York: Morrow.

1, 2, Buckle My Shoe. 1993. Illus. by L. Loveless. New York: Hyperion.

Roll Over! A Counting Song. 1981. Illus. by M. Peek. Boston: Houghton Mifflin.

This Old Man. 1990. Illus. by C. Jones. Boston: Houghton Mifflin.

The Twelve Days of Christmas. 1990. Illus. by J. Brett. New York: Putnam.

Wadsworth, O.A. 1985. *Over in the Meadow*. Illus. by E.J. Keats. New York: Scholastic.

_____. 1992. *Over in the Meadow: An Old Counting Rhyme*. Illus. by D.A. Carter. New York: Scholastic.

Collections That Contain Several Counting-Out Rhymes, Songs, and Chants (All P)

Charles, F. 1996. *A Caribbean Counting Book*. Illus. by R. Arenson. Boston: Houghton Mifflin.

Cole, J. & S. Calmenson, eds. 1991. *The Eentsy, Weentsy Spider: Fingerplays and Action Rhymes*. Illus. by A. Tiegreen. New York: Morrow.

_____. 1990. *Miss Mary Mack and Other Children's Street Rhymes*. Illus. by A. Tiegreen. New York: Morrow.

Hall, N.A. & J. Syverson-Stork, eds. 1994. *Los Pollitos Dicen/The Baby Chicks Sing: Traditional Games, Nursery, Rhymes, and Songs from Spanish Speaking Countries*. Illus. by K. Chorao. Boston: Little, Brown.

Most, B. 1990. *Four & Twenty Dinosaurs*. New York: Four Winds.

Schwartz, A. sel. 1992. *And the Green Grass Grew All Around: Folk Poetry for Everyone*. New York: HarperCollins.

Yolen, J. sel. 1992. *Street Rhymes Around the World*. Honesdale, PA: Wordsong.

Authors and illustrators sometimes use the conventions of counting and numbers as an organizing device for creating beautiful art or for conveying information. Examples of these counting books can be brought into the classroom for children to categorize and explore. One group of first-graders found counting books with places (such as *One White Sail: A Caribbean Counting Book* and *Uno, Dos, Tres: One, Two, Three*, a counting book set in a Mexican market) and counting books about animals (such as *Counting Cranes* and *Pigs from One to 10*) among the books they reviewed.

After the children had noticed that some books counted beyond ten, their teacher suggested that the students look in the books to see which numbers were included. Denise Fleming's *Count!* includes the numbers one to ten and then counts by tens to fifty, and E.J. Pinczes' *Arctic Fives Arrive* counts by fives. Some books contain countdowns, such as Molly Bang's *Ten, Nine, Eight*, William Wise's *Ten Sly Piranhas*, and the counting song "Ten in a Bed." After sorting the books, the children might make a chart to show other class members what numbers were in each of the books. Other children might want to use some

cated to "P.C.T.—whom I know I can always count on." In this book, a young girl counts all of her buddies as a way of counting her blessings. The book contains a section, "For Adults and Kids," with ideas that include counting objects in the pictures, counting backward, counting friends, and counting when cooking, shopping, or taking a walk.

A number of counting books exist on several levels, showing beginners the rudiments of counting, but also exploring more complex applications. In Seymour Chwast's *The 12 Circus Rings*, a cumulative story, certain numbers of each object appear in the rings. Pages in the back expand on the simple counting concept by asking such questions as, "How many people and animals are there in the entire circus?" Another page shows some interesting patterns among numbers in the various rings and suggests children look for others. In *The M&M's Brand Chocolate Candies Counting Book* and *The Cheerios Counting Book*, the first exercises in counting are quite simple, but they become increasingly complex.

Some books encourage us to take counting beyond the subject of mathematics books. Counting books on various topics can be fitted into science and social studies and provide models for students' own writings about the new knowledge they have acquired. Because dedications and titles in math books sometimes include some of the common phrases we use involving math and numbers, such as "everybody counts," "a person you can count on," and "one in a million," students might want to explore some of the other phrases that involve numbers. Heidi Goennel's *Odds and Evens: A Numbers Book* counts from one to thirteen, with a cliche for each of the numbers, such as "two in the bush" and "behind the eight ball." Percival Everett's *The One That Got Away* is a western tall tale that plays with the several ways we use the word *one* in the English language.

Children might also be interested to learn that researchers are studying animals to see if they can count. Marjory Facklam includes a chapter, "Count on It" in *What Does the Crow Know? The Mysteries of Animal Intelligence*, and Ali Wakefield's *Those Calculating Crows* tells of an experiment done by hunters some years ago. "A Note About the Story" at the beginning explains that crows can't count to ten, but they can count to seven. The story tells of a farmer who tries to trick the birds by staying in the barn as a cumulation of relatives and friends leave one by one, but the crows seem to figure out that not everyone is gone.

Counting and Numbers Across the Curriculum

Atherly, S. 1995. *Math in the Bath (And Other Fun Places, Too!)* Illus. by M. Halsey. New York: Simon & Schuster. (P)
See text.

Chwast, S. 1993. *The 12 Circus Rings.* San Diego: Harcourt Brace. (P)
See text.

Everett, P. 1992. *The One That Got Away.* Illus. by D. Zimmer. New York: Clarion. (U/P)
See text.

Facklam, M. 1994. "Count on It." In *What Does the Crow Know? The Mysteries of Animal Intelligence.* Illus. by P. Johnson. San Francisco: Sierra Club. (U/P)
See text.

Goennel, H. 1994. *Odds and Evens: A Numbers Book.* New York: Tambourine. (U/P)
See text.

McGrath, B.B. 1998. *The Cheerios Counting Book.* Illus. by B. Bolster & F. Mazzola, Jr. New York: Scholastic. (P)
See text.

———. 1994. *The M&M's Brand Chocolate Candies Counting Book.* Watertown, MA: Charlesbridge. (P)
See text.

Murphy, S.J. 1997. *Every Body Counts.* Illus. by F. Dunbar. New York: HarperCollins. (P)
See text.

Wakefield, A. 1996. *Those Calculating Crows.* Illus. by C. Hale. New York: Simon & Schuster. (U)
See text.

Teaching Mathematics with a Communication Model

Teachers who want children to understand mathematical concepts and to communicate their understanding have always embraced a learning model that is *individual, interactive,* and *integrative* (Moffett & Wagner 1992). We believe, like Moffett and Wagner, that children bring personal experiences—background knowledge, attitudes, and ways of learning—to the mathematics classroom. Children need an opportunity to compare their thinking with others, to collaborate in problem-solving activities, and to communicate their insights, both orally and in writing. Good language arts teachers and mathematics teachers are interested in both process and product. Teachers who want children to be confident and skillful mathematicians know that several things must happen.

First, an environment that is conducive to a certain kind of learning must be created. This includes the physical environment as well as the psychological environment. The arrangement of the room is one that invites talk, movement, discovery, and the full involvement of students. It is crisscrossed by almost visible lines of trust (Romano 1987). In this environment, teachers model their thinking, writing, and problem-solving strategies, communicating their thoughts, struggles, and insights out loud. Within the same environment, children build on what they know, gain confidence in themselves as mathematicians, and probe their own thinking processes. Through reading, writing, speaking, listening, and viewing, children construct mathematics for themselves.

Second, mathematics instructors who embrace a communication model realize that children need an opportunity to grapple with a concept as well as a way to express their questioning, confirming, and understanding of it. Many would agree with middle school mathematics instructor Victor Wilkerson, who uses writing as a key tool for thinking in mathematics. Mr. Wilkersen explains, "When students write, whether it is in English or in math, they do many things. Probably the most important thing that they do is think. Writing requires them to look at their thoughts and ideas in a given subject and analyze them" (Wilkerson 1997).

Language and Large Numbers

How might a teacher use the language operations of reading, writing, speaking, listening, and viewing to teach the mathematical concept of large numbers to upper elementary students? To introduce the concept, we might begin by reading a picture book. In *How Much Is a Million?* by David N. Schwartz, readers see right away the connection between words and numbers in Schwartz's dedication: "For Mom and Dad who started me on the little numbers; for Judy who made me pick up the pace, and for Mary Lou who is one in a million." In this picture book, many "if" statements describe the space and size of a million, a billion, and a trillion. The book includes notes and activities on measurement of large numbers, capacity, and counting stars. After listening to the book, children might enjoy constructing their own counting books, using large numbers.

Sometimes a provocative real-world example can involve students in discussions of the abstract concept of large numbers. One fourth-grade teacher said to his class, "There was a car salesman named Bill who told me he had a million cars on his lot. We've been working on our number sense and have been learning that one million is a truly big number. I'm a little skeptical of Bill. How about you?"

The class agreed with their teacher. To prove to Bill what a big number a million was, the class decided to show him what a million small cars would look like. The teacher drew one car. He explained that if you put ten of them together, you have ten cars; if you put ten of those together, you have one hundred cars; if you put ten of those together, you have one thousand cars. Depicting each addition with a page of miniature cars created on the computer, the instructor showed the children what a million looked like. The display of a million tiny automobiles filled two walls and confirmed the children's skepticism about Bill.

In a similar activity, a fourth-grade teacher helped her students to understand large numbers and place value by role playing. She selected the number 198,975 and had seven students represent it. One student held a sign holding the five, indicating the ones place; another held a sign with a seven, holding the tens place; a third held a nine, marking the hundreds place; and so on until each number and its place value was enacted, including the comma. The children read the number aloud and then traded places to create variations on the number.

A student teacher in the same classroom extended the role playing activity by using the populations of the ten largest cities in the United States. She began the lesson by asking students to guess what the largest cities were. As they guessed correctly, she held up a sign with the name of the city and its population figure. She reported that the fourth-graders guessed the top ten cities quite easily. With the ten cities randomly displayed across the chalkboard tray, the student teacher asked volunteers to rearrange the ten sheets of construction paper, ranking the cities from the largest to the smallest. After much discussion and revision, the children agreed that the cities were ranked correctly. Then she asked students to name the largest city that had a two in the thousands place, a four in the hundreds place, a one in the millions place, and so on.

As an extension activity, the teacher formed teams, giving each team two sets of construction paper squares containing the numbers zero to nine and two commas. Each group was challenged to make the largest number possible with a six in the hundreds place, a nine in the thousands place, a seven in the ten thousands place, and so on. The children moved the numbers around, revised their answers, and remembered where the commas went. After playing the game, they were asked to write for ten minutes about large numbers. How were they formed? How did they rank order the cities from the largest to smallest? Was any aspect tricky for them?

These students used reading, writing, speaking, listening, and dramatic activities to explore the concept of large numbers; they demonstrated their learning orally and in writing; they hypothesized, confirmed their guesses, and used writing-to-learn to reflect on the lesson in a ten-minute freewrite; the students arranged and rearranged numbers, negotiated solutions with group members, and represented large numbers visually. An activity that brings such a unit full circle is to go back to the published books on mathematics. Students might work with the school librarian to look for picture books that could be used to teach math concepts, categorizing books that teach place value, large numbers, and money, as well as skills for younger children, such as counting and addition and subtraction. There's a good chance David M. Schwartz's second book, *If You Made a Million*, dealing with large amounts of money, might show up on someone's list, which is an opportunity to look at large numbers in relation to banking, interest income, and appreciation.

Large Numbers

Anno, M. 1983. *Anno's Mysterious Multiplying Jar*. New York: Putnam. (U)
Using illustrations of everyday objects, Anno presents problems that students can solve to better understand factorials.

Clement, R. 1991. *Counting on Frank*. Milwaukee: Gareth Stevens. (P)
As he and his dog go through their day, a boy calculates large numbers of unusual items, such as what if a mosquito were four million times larger.

Demi. 1997. *One Grain of Rice*. New York: Scholastic. (P)
Rani asks the cruel emperor for one grain of rice, doubled every day for thirty days, in this Indian tale about wisdom and large numbers.

McKissack, P. 1992. *A Million Fish More or Less*. Illus. by D. Schutze. New York: Knopf. (P)

Hugh-Thomas tells a tall tale of catching a million fish, more or less, in
this picture book set on the bayou.

Schwartz, D.M. 1985. *How Much Is a Million?* Illus. by S. Kellogg.
New York: Lothrop. (U/P)
See text.

_____. 1989. *If You Made a Million*. Illus. by S. Kellogg. New York:
Lothrop. (U/P)
See text.

Wild, M. 1984. *Something Absolutely Enormous*. New York: Scholastic. (P)
In a brief book that may spur student writings on the consequences of
and uses for enormous things, Sally knits "something absolutely enormous" that is later used as a circus tent, then begins to bake "something
absolutely enormous."

Assessments of Mathematics Using Language

By exploring materials, recording their explorations, and formulating
new questions, by "measuring things in words," as Richards has termed
it, the children used language to learn like mathematicians (Richards
1990). A by-product was the visibility of their levels of understanding.
By visiting with students and by looking at their written records, it was
easy for the teachers to assess their children's learning.

Assessment records, in addition to entries made in logs or letters,
might include summaries of the information learned, student-made
books, personal definitions of mathematical terms, lists of questions, and
student-generated games. Whenever students can transfer a concept
from one form to another, learning has occurred. For example, children
who create accurate visual representations of a concept, dramatize it effectively, put it to music, or publish or perform a concept successfully
demonstrate their understanding of it. Students who have made sense of
a concept can put it in their own words, illustrations, or lyrics. They
understand the concept, and it can be built on throughout the year.

Loreen Leedy's *Measuring Penny* provides a vivid example of a cumulative activity that assesses children's knowledge of a topic in mathematics (Leedy 1998). When Lisa's teacher gives an assignment that
his students measure something, and to be imaginative in their choice,
she decides to measure her dog, Penny, including comparisons to other
dogs. Her measurements include relative length of noses in inches and
centimeters, ears measured in cotton swabs, tails measured in dog bis-
cuits, sitting and standing heights, length of Penny's jump, volume of

Chapter Five

Just Look
Observing the World Around Us as Scientists and Creative Writers

Writing About Science

Scientists and writers are investigators. Both are involved in careful consideration of the world around them; both are explorers, observing and formulating ideas about what they see. Too often, though, our curriculum doesn't reflect linkages between subjects like science and writing, and we limit children by assigning certain types of writing to certain subjects. We ask children to write informatively for science lessons and creatively in language arts. However, if we look at books on science and nature for children, we discover that neither scientists nor writers have such constraints. Poets observe nature through the eyes of scientists, describing what they experience in careful sensory detail. Byrd Baylor, for example, reveals much about nature in the American Southwest while showing reverent respect for its inhabitants in her free-verse books, *Desert Voices* (1993) and *I'm in Charge of Celebrations* (1986). Scientist Ron Hirschi writes poetically about the natural world in his books about the ecosystems of the northern parts of our country, *Winter* and *Faces in the Mountains*. The enormous popularity of the *Magic School Bus* books, which combine accurate information with cartoon illustrations and a humorous narrative text, demonstrates that lively writing and art can convey information effectively.

Writing teacher Toby Fulwiler suggests that "student learning and writing abilities will both improve when teachers in all subject areas recognize the unique power of language to generate, develop, express, and communicate ideas about anything to anybody" (Fulwiler 1983, 22). When nonfiction books featuring a variety of styles of writing and presentation of information are available and when they are shared along with fiction and poetry during read-aloud sessions, they affect the quality and the diversity of student writings.

Some books provide rules or guides for exploring a subject. Students have enjoyed writing their own rules for finding a particular type of bird, a favorite pond, or river by using Byrd Baylor's *Everybody Needs a Rock*, with its rules for finding a rock, as a guide. Faith McNulty's *How to Dig a Hole to the Other Side of the Earth* provides a model for writing exact directions for a scientific exploration. Shirley Neitzel's *The House I'll Build for the Wrens* uses the cadences of *This Is the House That Jack Built* to show careful directions on how to build a birdhouse. Jim Arnosky's *Crinkleroot Guides* feature hand-printed and simply illustrated charts that students might want to try to make. These science guides, some humorous, some poetic, and some serious, suggest that this type of careful observation and recording of procedures is a necessary aspect of scientific investigation. When students have the opportunity to write procedures, rules, and guidebooks, they practice the literacy of science.

A number of authors and illustrators have used the organizational structures of alphabet books and other concept books to describe a field in science. Patricia Mullins' *V for Vanishing: An Alphabet of Endangered Species* and Diana Pomeroy's *Wildflower ABC* are examples of this type of organizational structure. Younger children may want to work collectively on an alphabet book that shows what they have learned about animals, plants, birds, or insects. Older students could create their own alphabets about more complex scientific concepts, such as ecosystems or studies of space.

Young writers and artists might want to create photo essays or illustrated essays that explore a concept or process in science. They might want to capture in pictures and text a project their class or school has undertaken to care for the environment. Molly Cone's *Come Back Salmon* and Bruce McMillan's *Nights of the Pufflings* feature photographs of children participating in such projects and could be used as models. They might want to create books or pictures that show a subject in science from a new perspective. Steve Jenkins' *Looking Down*, which shows the tiny earth from the perspective of space, or books that feature cutaway drawings are models of this type of work. A humorous perspective on science occurs in *Bottoms Up! A Book About Rear Ends*, which describes some strange features birds, fish, and animals have that help to protect them.

Student writers could also create dictionaries, detective stories (see Chapter Two for other ideas on this topic), diaries or journals (see Chapter Three for more ideas on this topic), or books organized around the seasons to show what they know about the topics in science that they are exploring. Scrapbooks (see Chapter Six for more on this subject) provide another possible way of expressing this knowledge. When young writers draw on these and other styles used in nonfiction literature, they create works that both inform and entertain.

Unique Styles of Writing Science

Guidebooks and Rules

Arnosky, J. 1990. *Crinkleroot's Guide to Walking in Wild Places*. New York: Simon & Schuster. (U/P)

_____. 1997. *Crinkleroot's Guide to Knowing the Birds*. New York: Simon & Schuster. (U/P)

_____. 1997. *Crinkleroot's Guide to Knowing Animal Habitats*. New York: Simon & Schuster. (U/P)
See text.

Baylor, B. 1974. *Everybody Needs a Rock*. Illus. by P. Parnall. New York: Simon & Schuster. (U/P)
See text.

McNulty, F. 1979. *How to Dig a Hole to the Other Side of the Earth*. Illus. by M. Simont. New York: HarperCollins. (P)
See text.

Nietzel, S. 1997. *The House I'll Build for the Wrens*. Illus. by N.W. Parker. New York: Greenwillow. (P)
See text.

Alphabet and Other Concept Books

Darling, K. 1996. *Amazon ABC*. Illus. by T. Darling. New York: Lothrop. (P)
Color photographs of animals of the Amazon are labeled, encouraging alphabetic arrangements of animals in other regions.

MacDonald, S. 1994. *Sea Shapes*. San Diego: Harcourt Brace. (P)
Cut-paper illustrations help readers to see ocean shapes, from stars to crescents, and notes about ocean creatures make this useful in art or science activities.

Mullins, P. 1993. *V for Vanishing: An Alphabet of Endangered Species*. New York: HarperCollins. (U/P)
Collage illustrations of endangered animals in alphabetical order include scientific names and the places they live.

Owens, M.B. 1988. *A Caribou Alphabet*. Brunswick, ME: Dogear Press. (U/P)
Rhymed text and illustrations interwoven with letters of the alphabet describe the habitat and behavior of the caribou.

_____. 1993. *Counting Cranes*. Boston: Little, Brown. (U/P)
A natural history of whooping cranes is presented, with counting used as an organizational device.

Pomeroy, D. 1997. *Wildflower ABC: An Alphabet of Potato Prints*. San Diego: Harcourt Brace. (U/P)
Varieties of wildflowers presented in alphabetical order might spark science or art activities.

Ruurs, M. 1996. *A Mountain Alphabet*. Illus. by A. Kiss. Plattsburgh, NY: Tundra. (U/P)
Paintings filled with natural things found in the mountains, beginning with each letter of the alphabet, as well as detailed notes help readers to explore the mountain ecosystem.

Ryden, H. 1996. *ABC of Crawlers and Flyers*. New York: Clarion. (U/P)
Close-up color photographs and brief text present twenty-six insects.

Thornhill, J. 1988. *The Wildlife ABC: A Nature Alphabet Book*. New York: Simon & Schuster. (P)

_____. 1989. *The Wildlife 123: A Nature Counting Book*. New York: Simon & Schuster. (P)
The alphabet and numbers are used as organizational tools in these books featuring brief, rhymed text and framed illustrations along with "Nature notes" on the animals portrayed.

Photo Essays/Books Illustrating a Process

Bang, M. 1996. *Chattanooga Sludge*. San Diego: Harcourt Brace. (U)
Elaborate collages and diagrams show the processes used to rid the Chattanooga River of pollution.

Cone, M. 1992. *Come Back, Salmon*. Illus. by S. Wheelwright. Boston: Houghton Mifflin. (U/P)
See text.

Hirschi, R. 1990. *Winter*. Illus. by T. Mangelsen. New York: Dutton. (U/P)

———. 1997. *Faces in the Mountains*. Illus. by T. Mangelsen. New York: Dutton. (U/P)

See text.

McMillan, B. 1995. *Nights of the Pufflings*. Boston: Houghton Mifflin. (U/P)

See text.

Different Perspectives

Clifford, N. 1996. *Incredible Earth*. New York: DK. (U)

This book and others in the Inside Guides series contain cutaways and three-dimensional models, close-ups, and small amounts of text to introduce readers to the cores and cross sections of natural and manufactured items.

Hirst, R. & S. Hirst. 1988. *My Place in Space*. Illus. by R. Harvey & J. Levine. New York: Orchard. (U/P)

When asked their address while boarding a bus, two children name addresses from their house, city, country, planet, and all the way to the universe.

Jenkins, S. 1995. *Looking Down*. New York: Ticknor and Fields. (U/P)

See text.

Parker, S. 1992. *Inside the Whale and Other Animals*. Illus. by T. Dewan. New York: Doubleday. (U)

Cutaway drawings reveal the anatomy of a number of the world's creatures.

Singer, M. 1997. *Bottoms Up! A Book About Rear Ends*. Illus. by P. O' Brien. New York: Henry Holt. (P)

See text.

Other Forms of Writing About Science

Highwater, J. 1995. *Songs for the Seasons*. Illus. by S. Speidel. New York: Lothrop. (U)

A free-verse exploration of the seasons focuses on red-tailed hawks and the interconnections among all of nature.

Leedy, L. 1993. *Postcards from Pluto: A Tour of the Solar System*. New York: Holiday. (U/P)

An imaginary field trip through the solar system features hand-printed postcards from the students about what they have seen.

Otten, C.F. 1997. *January Rides the Wind: A Book of Months*. Illus. by T.L.W. Doney. New York: Lothrop. (P)

Free-verse descriptions and illustrations of the months feature seasonal changes and activities.

Selsam, M.E. 1995. *How to Be a Nature Detective*. Illus. by M.H. Donnelly. New York: HarperCollins. (P)

Selsam shows that discovering which animals live in a place and what they do there is a type of nature detective work.

Simon, S. 1979. *Animal Fact/Animal Fable*. New York: Crown. (U/P)
This series of questions and answers about animal behavior (e.g., Are owls wise?) might provoke research and writing into other folklore about animals.

———. 1995. *Earth Words: A Dictionary of the Environment*. Illus. by M. Kaplan. New York: HarperCollins. (U)
This comprehensive dictionary of environmental terms is a useful reference for classroom study.

———. 1998. *They Swim the Seas: The Mystery of Animal Migration*. Illus. by E. Warnick. San Diego: Harcourt Brace. (U)
An exploration of scientific detectives who follow ocean animal migration patterns to discover how and why they move where they do.

Keeping Scientific Journals

While we want our students to express what they know in meaningful ways, we must first help them to learn about the world around them so that they have raw material for their writing. All knowledge begins in wonder. Too often we turn the study of science into simply memorization of facts, forgetting the power of science to delight and amaze us; we overlook its links with social studies, art, and language. One method of exploring links across disciplines is to encourage students to keep scientific journals.

In many classrooms, students record their scientific observations of a natural event or change process in journals. Books of poetry, fiction, and science books all model such practices (Chatton & Collins 1995). Paul Fleischman's poem, "Chrysalis Diary," for example, includes entries from the diary of a caterpillar undergoing metamorphosis. While the text takes the form of a poem and includes personification of the feelings of the caterpillar, the description of the processes through time is factual. Irene Brady's picture book, *Wild Mouse*, describes the daily events in the life of a mother mouse and her babies and models this scientific process. Brady records the times of her observations and documents through words and tiny drawings what she sees, hears, smells, and touches. Brady includes speculative questions, exploring possible explanations for what has occurred. She does not personify the mice, nor does she record her emotional reactions to having mice residing in her house.

Science Diaries, Journals, Logs, and Scrapbooks

Brady, I. 1976. *Wild Mouse*. New York: Scribners. (U/P)

See text.

Cole, J. 1992. *The Magic School Bus on the Ocean Floor*. Illus. by B. Degen. New York: Scholastic. (P)

This book and others in the *Magic School Bus* Series use cartoon bullets, school reports, amusing illustrations, and a narrative text to convey a great deal of information in this series of "field trips" on the Magic School Bus.

Ehlert, L. 1991. *Red Leaf, Yellow Leaf*. San Diego: Harcourt Brace. (P)

Simple text and collage and cutaway illustrations describe the planting and growth of trees and provide activities students can do in science and art.

———. 1995. *Snowballs*. San Diego: Harcourt Brace. (P)

In a format similar to that of *Red Leaf, Yellow Leaf*, Ehlert explores snow and snow activities with young children.

English, J.A. & T.D. Jones. 1996. *Mission Earth: Voyage to the Home Planet: Journals of an Astronaut and an Earth Observer*. New York: Scholastic. (U)

Using photographs taken in space, this journal, written aboard the space shuttle, emphasizes the work of astronauts and their feelings about their job.

Fleischman, P. 1988. "Chrysalis Diary." In *Joyful Noise*. Illus. by E. Beddowes. New York: HarperCollins. (U)

See text.

Frasier, D. 1998. *Out of the Ocean*. San Diego: Harcourt Brace. (U/P)

This tour of the ocean and beaches of Florida includes collages of sand, shells, photographs, and other beach artifacts.

George, J.C. 1959. *My Side of the Mountain*. New York: Dutton. (U)

Sam keeps a journal of his thoughts and observations when he spends a summer alone in the wilderness, with only animals for company.

———. 1997. *Look to the North: A Wolf Pup Diary*. Illus. by L. Washburn. New York: HarperCollins. (U/P)

The birth and growth of a wolf are described in this picture book, which could be paired with George's *Julie of the Wolves* or stand on its own.

Krupinski, L. 1994. *A New England Scrapbook: A Journey Through Poetry, Prose, and Pictures*. New York: HarperCollins. (U/P)

The question, "What is New England?" is answered in a variety of ways in this book, which might model works on other regions of study.

———. 1997. *Into the Woods: A Woodland Scrapbook*. New York: HarperCollins. (U/P)

Nature facts, lore, and legends are conveyed through hand-printed text and small drawings that model nature journals for young writers and artists.

Robbins, K. 1998. *Autumn Leaves*. New York: Scholastic. (U/P)
Photographs of leaves (in their actual sizes) and the trees from which they fall invite readers to create their own leaf collections.

Silver, D.M. 1997. *One Small Square Swamp*. Illus. by P.J. Wynne. New York: McGraw-Hill. (U/P)
This book and others in the *One Small Square* Series feature drawings, notebook pages, and projects to do when studying ecosystems.

While acting as scientists, students need to be as objective as Irene Brady in *Wild Mouse*. But emotional reactions, when coupled with close observation, are powerful tools for student writers. A three-column journal that separates objective observations from speculation and personal feelings can help students organize their thoughts. Column One features observations and may include drawings. Column Two might be devoted to speculation about the meaning of things observed and questions that still need to be answered. Column Three might contain emotional responses to the events being observed.

After reading Beverly Cleary's *Henry Huggins*, in which Henry obtains some guppies from the pet store and then has to deal with a population explosion, a group of third-grade readers observed some guppies in their classroom. They kept science journals, modeled after Brady's book, that included the date and time of each observation, the number of guppies, their relative size, the changes in the water in the aquarium, the amount of food consumed, and so on. The students included their questions and ideas in the second column of their journals: Why did the number of fish change so fast? Why do fish need to reproduce so rapidly? After the "population explosion," why did the fish begin to die? The children's emotional reactions to these events were recorded in the third column: the excitement of the expanding numbers of fish, followed by shock at finding the declining numbers and grief at the deaths of certain fish who had been identified by certain characteristics and names.

Lists and Catalogues

Writing can emerge from any column in the journal. A form of poetry that might emerge from Column One is a catalogue or list poem. In this type of free verse, the poet lists the attributes of a particular creature, topic, or event. Christopher Smart's poem, "My Cat, Jeoffrey," for example, describes each of Jeoffrey's behaviors, from his walk, to his bathing, to his purr. Similarly, Rosalie Moore's "Catalog" describes the ways that cats move and sit, talk and sleep. Young scientists can also observe physiological differences between creatures and catalogue them in list poems, as Marilyn Singer does in her poems "Ears" and "Tails," which compare dogs' ears and tails.

Lists and Catalogues of Natural Things

Brown, M.W. 1947. *The Important Book*. New York: HarperCollins. (P)
Simple descriptions of objects and natural phenomena include one aspect that is "the important thing," inviting children to make their own collections of important things.

Conrad, P. 1995. *Animal Lingo*. Illus by B.B. Falk. New York: HarperCollins. (U/P)
With its descriptions of the sounds animals in other countries make (e.g., in Israel, turkeys say "holderolderal" instead of "gobble"), this book invites research into other languages.

De Regniers, B.S. 1985a. "Some Things I Know About Cats." In *This Big Cat and Other Cats I've Known*. Illus. by A. Daniel. Westminster, MD: Crown. (U/P)

————. 1985b. "A Special Dictionary to Help You Understand Cats." In *This Big Cat and Other Cats I've Known*. Illus. by A. Daniel. Westminster, MD: Crown. (U/P)
Lists of cat qualities in these free-verse poems might encourage writers to list qualities of other favorite animals.

Lewis, J.P. 1990. "A Tomcat Is." In *A Hippopotamusn't*. Illus. by V. Chess. New York: Dial. (U/P)
A list of the roles played by a tomcat (e.g., "caretaker of naps") in the form of a rhymed poem.

Machotka, H. 1992. *Breathtaking Noses*. New York: Morrow. (P)
Photographs of noses encourage lists of other unique animal parts through pictures or words.

McMillan, B. 1992. *The Baby Zoo*. New York: Scholastic. (U/P)
The names of male, female, and young of many animals (e.g., stallion, mare, foal) encourage exploration of other animal names.

Moore, R. 1987. "Catalog." In *Cat Poems*, ed. M.C. Livingston. Illus. by T.S. Hyman. New York: Holiday. (U/P)
See text.

Riley, L. 1995. *Elephants Swim.* Illus. by S. Jenkins. Boston: Houghton Mifflin. (P)
  Two-word phrases describe the activities of a list of animals.
Singer, M. 1993. *It's Hard to Read a Map with a Beagle on Your Lap.* Illus. by C. Ouberie. New York: Holt. (U/P)
  See text.
Smart, C. 1992. *My Cat Jeoffrey.* Illus. by M. Leman. New York: Pelham. (U)
  See text.

■■■■

Exploring Through Questions

Children can also write from Column Two of their science journal—the column that focuses on questions. In her collection, *Always Wondering*, Aileen Fisher includes poems full of questions about the world she observes around her: How do squirrels remember where they hide the seed cones they store? How do baby chicks figure out how to hatch? How do spiders keep so much thread inside of them? How do they know how to spin their webs? Speculative thinking—ideas about why nature works—is inherent in many poems. In *Who Shrank My Grandmother's House? Poems of Discovery*, Barbara Juster Esbensen includes poems that contain questions or speculations about geodes, starfish, and prisms, among others. These are the very questions scientists use to form hypotheses that are explored in their work.

■■■■

Questions in Literature

Esbensen, B.J. 1992. *Who Shrank My Grandmother's House? Poems of Discovery.* Illus. by E. Beddowes. New York: HarperCollins. (U)
  See text.
Fisher, A. 1991. *Always Wondering.* Illus. by J. Sandin. New York: HarperCollins. (P)
  See text.
Hoban, T. 1995. *Animal, Vegetable, Mineral?* New York: Greenwillow. (P)
  Photographs invite children to decide to which category an item might belong.
Hopkins, L.B., ed. 1992. *Questions.* Illus. by C. Crull. New York: HarperCollins. (P)
  A collection of simple poems, each with a question young children might have.

A Unit on Canada Geese

Children who are studying migration, for example, might choose sources about Canada geese and their migration each fall. Nancy White Carlstrom's free-verse picture book, *Goodbye Geese*, like the preceding lists of books and poems of questions, describes the exodus of the geese and the coming of winter with metaphorical questions and answers. Jane Yolen's poem, "Birdwatcher," presents both visual and sound images of the departure of the geese. In her longer poem, "Autumn Song of the Goose," Yolen gives the goose a human persona as it calls out to its mate. This poem parallels the fantasy of goose migration in Jane Langton's novel, *The Fledgling*. Joanne Ryder's free-verse picture book, *Catching the Wind*, gives a scientific insight into migration coupled with a sense of what it must be like to fly away. Picture books by Molly Bang, Patricia Polacco, and Jane Yolen tell stories about Canada geese as well. After looking at these sources, students can generate a web of questions to answer about their readings. These might include the following:

■ Which of these are "real" geese behaviors?
■ Which are human (personified) interpretations?
■ What do the poets and writers do to make the geese seem like humans?
■ Why do geese migrate?
■ Why do people see this behavior as important to them?

Canada Geese

Bang, M. 1996. *Goose*. New York: Blue Sky Press. (P)
   In this imaginative story with realistic illustrations, baby goose gets lost from its mother and finds that it can look for her by flying.
Carlstrom, N.W. 1992. *Goodbye Geese*. Illus. by E. Young. New York: Morrow. (U/P)
   See text.
George, K.O. 1997. "Canada Geese." In *The Great Frog Race and Other Poems*. New York: Clarion. (U/P)
   A simple poem focuses on the sounds of geese as they leave in the autumn.
Kinsey-Warnock, N. 1989. *The Canada Geese Quilt*. Illus. by L.W. Bowman. New York: Cobblehill. (P)
   A family quilt features a design of Canada geese.
Langton, J. 1980. *The Fledgling*. New York: HarperCollins. (U)

In this fantasy novel with an environmental theme, a girl who lives near Walden Pond works to save it with the help of a talking Canada goose.

Polacco, P. 1996. *I Can Hear the Sun: A Modern Myth.* New York: Philomel. (P)

In this modern interpretation of a classic story, a homeless boy is befriended by a blind goose and flies off to live with her flock.

Ryder, J. 1989. *Catching the Wind.* Illus. by M. Rothman. New York: Morrow. (U/P)

See text.

Sanfield, S. 1996. *The Girl Who Wanted a Song.* Illus. by S.T. Johnson. San Diego: Harcourt Brace. (P)

Inspired by the Ten Oxherding pictures of Zen Buddhism, this contemporary story tells of a grieving girl who befriends a lone Canadian goose and learns a lesson about singing and about flying.

Simont, M. 1997. *The Goose That Almost Got Cooked.* New York: Scholastic. (P)

In this story that reveals the differences between wild and domestic geese, a Canada goose drops out of its migrating flock to visit domestic geese in the farmyard and nearly becomes a goose dinner.

Yolen, J. 1986. "Autumn Song of the Goose." In *Ring of Earth.* Illus. by John Wallner. San Diego: Harcourt Brace. (U/P)

See text.

_____. 1990. "Birdwatcher." In *Birdwatch: A Book of Poetry.* Illus. by T. Lewin. New York: Putnam. (U/P)

See text.

_____. 1993. *Honkers.* Illus. by L. Baker. Boston: Little, Brown. (P)

In this picture book that might be paired with either of Yolen's poems on Canada geese, a lonely girl befriends a goose and learns from its migration that each of us must make the journey home.

A Unit on the Big Dipper

Almost any topic or concept that is part of our science curriculum can be viewed through the three aspects of the science journal, with close observations, questions, and personal reactions included as part of the study. In addition, any topic in science can be expanded to include other disciplines, genres, and forms. A unit on the Big Dipper, described here, begins with student questions and expands to include scientific, literary, historical, and musical perspectives.

A walk outside to look at the night skies provokes a number of questions. Some constellations, such as the Big and Little Dippers, shine brightly. A glance at these constellations might raise questions like these:

- Why are these groups of stars named the Big and Little Dippers?
- Who named them?
- Why is the Big Dipper sometimes called The Drinking Gourd?
- Why and how was The Drinking Gourd used as a guide by escaping slaves?
- Why are these groups of stars also called Ursa Major (Great Bear) and Ursa Minor (Little Bear). Where did their names come from? How can we learn to find these bears in the night sky?

Although the wondering begins in a science lesson on astronomy and stars, the questions move us into the study of differing visions of the night sky. In literary study, children might investigate the different ways people have wondered about the Big and Little Dippers. Books of Greek and Roman myths and legends will help them answer their questions about the Great and Little Bears. They tell the story of Juno, who was jealous of the maiden, Callisto, and turned her into a great bear, and of Jupiter, the king of the gods, who turned Callisto's son into a smaller bear and hurled them both into the heavens, where we see them each night. Because the powers of the ocean are close to Juno, Jupiter decreed that the bears would never fall below the seas, but would revolve high in the night sky. That is why we see them at all seasons of the year. From these stories, we have inherited the Latin names, Ursa Major and Minor for Great and Little Bear. A Greek legend involves Bootes, a runaway horse from Phaeton's chariot, who dragged a plough across the sky. Some modern Europeans, rather than seeing the shape of a bear, see a Great Plough or Great Wagon in the sky in an echo of this legend.

Children exploring American stories will discover that a number of Native American cultural groups also saw a bear in the sky. Monroe and Williamson's *They Dance in the Sky: Native American Star Myths* and Bruchac's *The Earth Under Sky Bear's Feet: Native American Poems of the Land* retell versions of these legends. A popular writing activity in schools asks students to write their own stories in which they create explanations for occurrences in the world around them. As teachers, we should consult Paul Goble's note in *Adopted by the Eagles*, which cautions us against having children write *Indian legends*. All cultures have attempted explanations of natural phenomena. Some of the stories we refer to as legends are actually part of people's living belief systems, not only those of Native Americans, but also those from Africa and India. If we want our students to try writing their own explanations for natural phenomena, we might use *pourquoi* stories as models. These explanation stories (*pourquoi* being the French word for "why") are without contemporary religious or spiritual significance.

Pourquoi Stories and Legends

Aardema, V. 1975. *Why Mosquitoes Buzz in People's Ears: A West-African Tale*. Illus. by L. Dillon & D. Dillon. New York: Dial. (P)
When gossipy mosquito starts a rumor that ends in the death of a baby owl, lion sentences mosquito to forever buzz harmlessly in people's ears.

Bryan, A. 1985. *The Cat's Purr*. New York: Simon & Schuster. (P)
A West Indian story about rat and cat's fight over a drum and where the drum ended up.

Forest, H. 1988. *The Baker's Dozen*. Illus. by S. Gaber. San Diego: Harcourt Brace. (P)
This illustrated version of a traditional colonial tale explains why bakers often put thirteen cookies in a dozen.

Geringer, L. 1995. *The Pomegranate Seeds: A Classic Greek Myth*. Illus. by L. Gore. Boston: Houghton Mifflin. (U/P)
In this Greek legend, Persephone is rescued from the underworld and the seasons begin on earth.

Goble, P. 1994. *Adopted by the Eagles*. New York: Simon & Schuster. (U/P)
See text.

Kellogg, S. 1984. *Paul Bunyan: A Tall Tale*. New York: Morrow. (P)
_____. 1986. *Pecos Bill*. New York: Morrow. (P)
Explanations for such natural phenomena as the Grand Canyon are provided in these American tall tales.

Kipling, R. 1991. *The Just-So Stories*. Illus. by D. Frampton. New York: HarperCollins. (U/P)
Kipling's classic stories of how the elephant's child got his long trunk and the camel his hump are included in this collection.

Rockwell, A. 1996. *The One-Eyed Giant and Other Monsters from the Greek Myths*. New York: Greenwillow. (U/P)
Explanations for human behaviors, natural phenomena, and animal lore are found in these myths.

Wood, A. 1996. *The Bunyans*. Illus. by D. Shannon. New York: Blue Sky. (P)
This fantasy elaboration of Paul's story includes a whole family of
Bunyans, who accomplish more large deeds.

Another story about the Big and Little Dippers is hidden in the traditional song, "The Drinking Gourd." Illustrations and explanations
that accompany the song in music books show that the Drinking
Gourd was another name for the Big Dipper. Books about slave revolts
and desertion by runaway slaves before the Civil War, such as Virginia
Hamilton's poetic *Many Thousand Gone: African-Americans from Slavery to Freedom* and William Katz's and Walter Dean Myers' historical
texts, tell the stories of some of these heroic journeys. It was not the
constellation itself, but the fact that the two stars at the end of the
bowl of the Big Dipper pointed to Polaris, the North Star, in the handle
of the Little Dipper that was important. The North Star, long used by
sailors to find true north was what runaways searched for in the night
skies, and the Drinking Gourd was a term used to disguise the nature
of what they sought. The Drinking Gourd was one of a number of signs
used on the underground railroad. Histories reveal that the skies of the
south and east coasts were often cloudy or rainy, making guidance by
the stars impossible. The words to the song actually contain clues to
guides other than the stars, including people, such as Harriet Tubman;
physical landmarks, such as rivers and open areas; moss on the sides of
trees; and other signs of true north.

Studying the Big Dipper

Belting, N. 1966. *The Stars Are Silver Reindeer*. Illus. by E. Nesbitt.
New York: Holt. (U/P)
This collection features legends that explain the significance of a number
of constellations, including the Big Dipper.
Branley, F. 1991. *The Big Dipper*. New York: HarperCollins. (P)
A history and science of the constellation for younger children, this book
is part of the Let's Read and Find Out Science Series.
Bruchac, J. 1995. *The Earth Under Sky Bear's Feet: Native American Poems of
the Land*. New York: Philomel. (U/P)
A free-verse poem in this collection retells the Mohawk legend of the
Sky Bear.

Connelly, B. 1993. *Follow the Drinking Gourd: A Story of the Underground Railroad*. Illus. by Y. Buchanan. New York: Rabbit Ears/Simon & Schuster. (U/P)

This story, based on the legend of the Drinking Gourd, is enhanced by a CD with Morgan Freeman's narration and music by Taj Mahal.

Demi. 1996. *The Dragon's Tale and Other Animal Fables of the Chinese Zodiac*. New York: Holt. (U/P)

Stories of the beasts in the Chinese zodiac reveal another culture's view of star formations, and might lead to further study of how people see images in the stars.

Goble, P. 1988. *Her Seven Brothers*. New York: Simon & Schuster. (P)

Goble retells and illustrates the Cherokee legend of a courageous young woman and her brothers, who become stars.

Hamilton, V. 1995. *Many Thousand Gone: African-Americans from Slavery to Freedom*. New York: Knopf. (U)

Nonfiction accounts of runaway slaves in this volume reveal the role of the Drinking Gourd in their escape toward the North.

Isaacs, A. 1994. *Swamp Angel*. Illus. by P.O. Zelinsky. New York: Dutton. (P)

Like her tall-tale brothers, the huge young woman in this story changes the landscape and even has a hand in creating the Big Dipper.

Krupp, E.C. 1989. *The Big Dipper and You*. New York: Morrow (U)

A science book for older readers gives a history of the discovery of and stories about this collection of stars.

Monroe, J.G. & R.A. Williamson. 1987. *They Dance in the Sky: Native American Star Myths*. Boston: Houghton Mifflin. (U/P)

Chapter Two, "The Celestial Bear: Stories of the Big Dipper," includes Micmac, Coeur d'Alene, Wasco, and Snohomish legends.

Winter, J. 1988. *Follow the Drinking Gourd*. New York: Knopf. (P)

A simple illustrated version of the traditional song, this book will appeal to younger readers.

■■■■■

By separating their different types of observations into three columns as they write in scientific journals, students learn to distinguish among facts, opinions, and emotional responses. But they can also experiment with the ways that writers actually combine these resources to generate different types of writings about their subjects. Newspaper articles, editorials, position statements, feature stories, illustrated picture books, poetry, collages, speeches, and other oral presentations emerge naturally from the combined information in the three columns.

Chapter Six

Textures of Things

Introduction

One of the earliest phrases we might have learned to read was "Do Not Touch." While this sign was intended to protect us from terrible consequences, it also cut us off from one of the most important ways of interacting with the world. While we rely heavily on our visual senses, most of us use our sense of touch hundreds of times a day for a variety of purposes. Is the bath water too hot? Dip in a finger tip to find out. Is the dog feeling ill? Check to see if her nose is cold. Is my hair standing on end? Run my hand through it without looking in the mirror. Each of these touching experiences gives us information that we need to carry out our daily activities. We also use our sense of touch out of curiosity. Is that a real apple, or is it made of wax? Are those flowers as soft and furry as they look? At these moments, our questions are answered simply through the sense of touch.

Sometimes our sense of touch *is* a warning system. We pick up a pan with a burning-hot handle and drop it quickly, as soon as we feel heat on our skin. We stay out in the snow too long and our noses, fingers, and toes begin to ache in warning. We caress a silky rose and get scratched by the thorns that protect it. Our body's sensory organs, with their revelations about pain, alert us to potential hazards. We learn to use pot holders, to dress warmly, and to pick roses with care because our sense of touch teaches us about these hazards.

At other times, our sense of touch provides pleasure. The cat jumps into our lap, kneading us gently with his paws while we run our hands down the soft fur of his back. We take off our shoes after a hot walk and stick our feet into the chilly river. That bath water we tested is now the perfect temperature and full of bubbles; we sink into it, feeling its warmth all over our skin.

Generally, the sense of touch is studied in the primary grades as part of units on the senses. But the sense of touch and its accompanying experience of texture can provide a framework for connections among science, art, and experiences in reading and writing across the grade levels. In one popular touch experience, students reach into a paper bag without looking, and using only their sense of touch and their prior knowledge of the texture and feel of objects, they make guesses about what it is they are touching. Sometimes they determine objects by their shape, such as buttons or safety pins. Sometimes the objects are determined by their texture, such as the feel of pine cones or sea urchins. Sometimes both shape and texture play a role in the solution to the mystery in the bag, such as when we try to guess if the object in the bag might be a lemon or an orange.

Poet Zaro Weil has taken such an exercise as the subject for her poem, "The Paper Bag" (Weil 1992). Her bag includes some things that are sounds: "spring sounds" and "winter quiet." Others are abstract qualities, such as "secrets." Her last hidden item is velvet, and she suggests you put it in the paper bag, "just to have it." What the poet does is take the experiential activity we often use in science lessons and suggest that the texture of something (in her case, velvet) is also an experience to treasure in itself. It is no accident that Weil also suggests that we can keep words in our bag, words that can be used to express our thoughts and feelings as we explore the textures of the world around us.

Textures of Rocks

In conjunction with this bag activity, children might be asked to practice descriptive words, creating lists of words that describe the texture of the items that they feel. This can be a difficult activity if students have not been exposed to literature that introduces them to the vocabulary of sensory language. Suppose we put a particular rock in our bag and web as a class some words that we could use to describe it. Typically, children will come up with words such as *hard, cool, smooth,* or *rough,* depending on the rock. While these are all good words, they are limited. What if we then read science and nature writers, poets, and writers looking at the ways they describe rocks, creating a web of words where we had only a few? Then we might think about the best words from all the rock words we've found to describe our class rock as we continue to explore rocks in science and literature. What the scientist and the poet know is that rocks are unique. The scientist might call our rock *igneous* simply from feeling its shape and texture. The poet might say it needs to be perfectly suited to us, as Byrd Baylor does in *Everybody Needs a Rock*, a book that suggests using our senses to find the right size, shape, and texture of a rock for our own hand.

After our rock-touching exercise, we might be moved to follow Byrd Baylor's rules and take an expedition to find perfect rocks for each of us to explore and write about. Or, we might collect examples of the various types of rocks described in our science books and label them with their rock descriptions. While many of us grew up with signs that said, "Do Not Touch," more and more museums and classrooms are creating centers that encourage exploration and experimentation through touching. "Please Touch" is a more common motto in exploratoriums, which, for example, allow students to feel static electricity, the fur of a seal, or a dinosaur bone.

Discovery learning centers in classrooms encourage students to find out by holding, touching, and manipulating objects and asking questions about their origins and purposes. In a rock unit, a center where rocks are collected, identified, and categorized by children is more meaningful than one where a commercial company has neatly sorted, labeled, and boxed these rocks for children to view. Those of us who simply memorize the names and forms of rocks will lose that information quickly. Those of us who searched for, analyzed, touched, and labeled specimens from our neighborhoods will remember those rocks and the reasons why they were where we found them.

As we gather rocks for both poetic and scientific descriptions, we continue to read about them in a variety of books, stories, and poems, writing and responding as we do so. We might look at famous rocks, such as Ayers Rock in the middle of Australia, or Devil's Tower, which looms above the Wyoming plains. These rocks have become the subject of stories and speculation because they are so different from the landscape that lies around them. We might look at the huge standing stones erected by people in Britain or on Easter Island, incredible feats of engineering in stone by ancient people. We might look at rocks in folk tales and fantasy—stones that are magical or that work magic in an ordinary way, as the rock in *Stone Soup* does. We can look at rocks in poetry and the ways they are described in picture books, stories, and novels, as well as in informational books. We might study rock art, exploring these stories on stone.

As we read, explore, and study, we continue to increase the vocabulary we can use to describe the experience of rocks. Our web of rock words expands, with branches that could include technical terms, scientific names, names of famous rocks, words from other languages and cultures, and so on. This *web dictionary* of rock names is available for our use with any poetry, stories, scientific, or historical writing we might choose to do.

Rocks Across the Curriculum

Legendary Rocks

Bruchac, J. 1996. "From a Friend . . ." In *Between Earth and Sky: Legends of Native American Sacred Places*. Illus. by Thomas Locker. San Diego: Harcourt Brace. (U)
A free-verse poem retells the Navajo story of El Capitan, a symbol of how good can overcome evil.

Morin, P. 1998. *Animal Dreaming: An Aboriginal Dreamtime Story*. Buffalo, NY: Stoddart. (U/P)
Paintings on wood emulate the rock art drawings that told this ancient aboriginal story.

Yolen, J. 1996a. "Stonehenge." In *Sacred Places*. Illus. by D. Shannon. San Diego: Harcourt Brace. (U)
This free-verse poem honors the Druids, who created Stonehenge.

————. 1996b. "Uluru." In *Sacred Places*. Illus. by D. Shannon. San Diego: Harcourt Brace. (U)
A free-verse poem to the monument we know as Ayers Rock, which remembers the dreamtime in Australia.

Rocks in Folk Tales

Goble, P. 1988. *Iktomi and the Boulder: A Plains Indian Story*. New York: Orchard. (P)
Iktomi, the trickster in Plains Indian lore, meets his match when he encounters a magic boulder.

Newton, P. 1990. *The Stonecutter*. New York: Putnam. (P)
A stonecutter wishes for wealth and power in this Indian folk tale, similar to the traditional western European story of the magic fish.

Stewig, J. 1991. *Stone Soup*. Illus. by M. Tomes. New York: Holiday. (P)
Trickery with a stone is used to encourage villagers to be generous with their food.

Yacowitz, C. 1992. *The Jade Stone: A Chinese Folktale*. Illus. by Ju-Hong Chen. New York: Holiday. (U/P)

This is a Mandarin tale of a stonecutter who *hears* the carp that wants to be carved inside a piece of jade. The stonecutter gets into trouble with the Emperor, who instead wants a carving of a dragon.

Rocks in Poetry

Baylor, B. 1975. *Everybody Needs a Rock*. Illus. by P. Parnall. New York: Simon & Schuster. (P)

See text.

Esbensen, B.J. 1992. "Geode." In *Who Shrank My Grandmother's House? Poems of Discovery*. Illus. by E. Beddows. New York: HarperCollins. (U/P)

The wonder of finding a tiny glittering "city" inside a stone is explored in this poem.

Lionni, L. 1961. *On My Beach There Are Many Pebbles*. New York: Morrow. (P)

This picture book invites beach walkers to take a closer look at the rocks on the beach to see what they really are.

McCord, D. 1993. "This Is My Rock." In *Secret Places*, ed. C. Huck. Illus. by L.B. George. New York: Greenwillow. (U/P)

McCord suggests in this poem that everyone needs a rock from which to survey and contemplate the world.

Marzollo, J. 1998. *I Am a Rock*. Illus. by J. Moffat. New York: Scholastic. (U/P)

Riddle poems feature common rocks, with questions that reveal their natural properties.

Worth, V. 1987a. "Pebbles." In *All the Small Poems*. Illus. by Natalie Babbitt. New York: Farrar, Straus & Giroux. (U/P)

———. 1987b. "Rocks." In *All the Small Poems*. Illus. by Natalie Babbitt. New York: Farrar, Straus & Giroux. (U/P)

These two small poems look carefully at the qualities of stones.

Rocks in Picture Books

Dunrea, O. 1998. *The Trow-Wife's Treasure*. New York: Farrar, Straus & Giroux. (P)

A farmer gets his wish from a circle of stone.

Lionni, L. 1974. *Alexander and the Wind-Up Mouse*. New York: Knopf. (P)

In this reversal of traditional stories, Alexander the mouse must find a purple pebble in order to get his wish to become more like a toy.

Noll, S. 1990. *Watch Where You Go*. New York: Puffin. (P)

A little mouse flees from danger, not knowing that the grass and rocks on which he runs are actually hidden animals.

Parnall, P. 1991. *The Rock*. New York: Macmillan. (P)

Lyrical language and simple line drawings are used to explore the life of a seemingly ordinary rock.

Patron, S. 1991. *Burgoo Stew*. Illus. by M. Shenan. New York: Orchard. (P)

A contemporary version of Stewig's *Stone Soup*, this story features an old man who tricks a group of boys.

Polacco, P. 1995. *My Ol' Man*. New York: Philomel. (P)

Polacco recalls a special summer spent in Michigan with her storytelling father, who shared with her the powers of a magical rock.

Steig, W. 1969. *Sylvester and the Magic Pebble*. New York: Simon & Schuster. (U/P)

Sylvester the donkey is mysteriously turned into a stone in this modern fantasy.

Swanson, S.M. 1998. *Letter to the Lake*. Illus. by P. Catalanotto. New York: DK Ink. (P)

Rosie's letter, which shares her memories of summer at the lake, describes the rocks she chose for tossing and her "best rock," shaped like a house, which she brought back home with her.

Van Allsburg, C. 1990. *The Wretched Stone*. Boston: Houghton Mifflin. (U/P)

In this fantasy told in the form of a ship's log, a ship's crew finds a strange glowing stone that nearly destroys them.

Rocks in Fiction

Clifton, L. 1979. *The Lucky Stone*. Illus. by D. Payson. New York: Delacorte. (U/P)

Tee and her great-grandmother tell stories about the lucky stone that has brought her family good fortune for generations.

Henkes, K. 1992. *Words of Stone*. New York: Greenwillow. (U)

When Blaze wakens to find a circle of stones made from the rocks he has symbolically buried after his mother's death, his life begins to change.

Hunter, M. 1996. *The Walking Stones*. San Diego: Harcourt Brace. (U)

A standing stone circle built by Druids in Scotland plays a role in this fantasy novel.

Wrightson, P. 1979. *The Nargun and the Stars*. New York: Atheneum. (U)

A huge creature that moves so slowly it resembles stone wreaks havoc on the Australian landscape in this fantasy novel.

Rocks in History

Fraser, M.A. 1994. *Sanctuary: The Story of Three Arch Rocks*. New York: Holt. (U)

The story of how America's first wildlife sanctuary on coastal rocks was established off of Oregon.

Fritz, J. 1975. *Who's That Stepping on Plymouth Rock?* Illus. by J.B. Handelsman. New York: Putnam. (U/P)

This humorous informational book describes the landing at Plymouth Rock and how this landmark has fared since then.

Macaulay, D. 1975. *Pyramid.* Boston: Houghton Mifflin. (U/P)

A fictional narrative is used to explore the mysteries of how the stone pyramids of Egypt were built.

Rocks in Geology

Cole, J. 1987. *Magic School Bus Inside the Earth.* Illus. by B. Degen. New York: Scholastic. (P)

In cartoon style, with many asides, this book explores the geologic formations deep inside the earth.

Gans, R. 1997. *Let's Go Rock Collecting.* New York: HarperCollins. (P)

This Let's Read and Find Out Series science book explains how different types of rocks were made and where to look for them.

Hiscock, B. 1988. *The Big Rock.* New York: Simon & Schuster. (P)

This book traces the history of an ancient piece of stone.

Hooper, M. 1996. *The Pebble in My Pocket: A History of Our Earth.* New York: Viking. (P)

The creation of a pebble is detailed from its time in a volcano and its use by cave people until it is found by modern children.

Jesperson, J. & J. Fitz-Randolph. 1996. *Mummies, Dinosaurs, Moon Rocks: How We Know How Old Things Are.* Illus. by B. Hiscock. New York: Atheneum. (U)

Scientific tests that have been developed to tell the age of ancient things, including old rocks, moon rocks, and meteors, are explored in this volume for older readers.

Other Means of Experiencing Texture

While touch with our hands is the most obvious way we explore texture, we can actually experience it in many ways. Mary O'Neill's poem, "Fingers Are Always Bringing Me News," suggests that "toes don't know because of shoes." Any child who has explored the world through his or her feet, knows that toes can experience a great deal of texture. Zilpha Snyder's "Poem to Mud," which describes the sensation of mud on one's toes, and

Aileen Fisher's "Going Barefoot," about the feeling of summer on your feet, provide examples of this sensation. Marilee Robin Burton's *My Best Shoes* is a gentle picture book that describes the sensations of various types of shoes but ends with going barefoot as the best pair of "shoes" to wear. Joanne Ryder's *Under Your Feet* encourages children to think about and feel the textures and sounds of the nature that lives under their feet.

Fiction also incorporates passages with textures on one's feet. Perhaps the most famous of these is the clear description of the feel of leeches on one's legs and feet in Laura Ingalls Wilder's *On the Banks of Plum Creek.* Similarly, in Lois Lowry's *Rabble Starkey,* Rabble and her friends Veronica and Gunther visit the warm creek on a September day and experience the slick feel of plants growing on the rocks in the bottom. Students may want to list other textures they experience through their feet, such as walking on sharp rocks on a hot summer road or the stinging feeling of stepping barefoot on an icy pavement. They may remember shocking experiences of walking on carpets to turn on a light and reflect on how the sensation of static passed through their feet, up through their bodies, and out their fingers in a spark of electricity.

Sometimes we can feel the textures of our own bodies and use them for descriptive writings. Sandra Cisneros' *Hairs/Pellitos* gives vivid descriptions, in both English and Spanish, of the colors and textures of hair in her family, and Natasha Anastasia Tarpley's picture book, *I Love My Hair,* describes all the different beautiful things about an African-American girl's curly hair. Joanne Ryder's poetic picture book, *My Father's Hands,* describes the texture of a father's hands and the small creatures he holds out for his daughter to touch as they work in the garden.

Texture is everywhere in the world around us. As we begin to pay attention to its sensations, we open ourselves to experiences in creative writing, science, and art. Exploring texture gives us a sensory experience that we can recreate as imagery in poetry and prose. It allows us to consider the range of textures in nature, in rocks, plants, and animals, experiences that can lead to scientific explorations of these surfaces. It gives us models for artistic expression as we play with texture in art.

Other Textures to Experience

Burton, M.R. 1994. *My Best Shoes.* Illus. by J.E. Ransom. New York:
  Tambourine. (P)
  See text.

Cisneros, S. 1994. *Hairs/Pellitos*. Illus. by T. Ybaniz. New York: Knopf. (P)
See text.

Fisher, A. 1961. *Going Barefoot*. New York: Crowell. (P)
See text.

Lowry, L. 1987. *Rabble Starkey*. Boston: Houghton Mifflin. (U)
See text.

O'Neill, M. 1969. *Fingers Are Always Bringing Me News*. New York: Doubleday. (U/P)
See text.

Ryder, J. 1994. *My Father's Hands*. Illus. by M. Graham. New York: Morrow. (P)
See text.

————. 1990. *Under Your Feet*. Illus. by D. Nolan. New York: Four Winds. (U/P)
See text.

Snyder, Z. 1969. "Poem to Mud." In *Today Is Saturday*. New York: Atheneum. (U/P)
See text.

Tarpley, N.A. 1998. *I Love My Hair*. Boston: Little, Brown. (P)
See text.

Wilder, L.I. 1937. *On the Banks of Plum Creek*. New York: HarperCollins. (U)
See text.

Experiencing Texture in Foods

One of the most pleasurable ways to experience the textures of things is through eating. Who has not enjoyed the tickle of soda pop bubbles on the roof of one's mouth, the soothing feel of peppermint on a sore, dry throat, or the delicious rumply texture of a potato chip melting on one's tongue?

From the time she was a small child, Barbara has craved smooth foods when she was troubled or upset. The comfort of chocolate pudding, applesauce, and smooth, liquidy macaroni and cheese eased the bumpy, prickly places in her life. For Barbara, it is the feeling of these smooth foods on her tongue, as much as the taste, that provides a sense of nurturing comfort. Because of her fondness for smooth foods and for foods in general, Barbara enjoys creating food sensory units with children when she visits classrooms to share poetry. And because of her fondness for chocolate in particular, she often shares passages from Richard Ammon's nonfiction book, *The Kids' Book of Chocolate*, which includes the natural history of chocolate and its manufacture, along with lots of other information.

She also shares a favorite poem, Arnold Adoff's "Love Song," a poem about chocolate in all of its textures, colors, and forms. One group of third-graders wrote a class poem with Barbara about their favorite food, ice cream. As they looked at Adoff's ways of describing chocolate, class members saw that texture was a key element in poems about ice cream. They included the phrase "It's creamy, it's cold, it's mushy, it's magnificent" in the class poem as a way of describing ice cream's texture.

Lots of foods are not smooth at all but are just as appealing. Eve Merriam's "In the Mood for Food" describes food textures, including the "lumpy, bumpy pickle." Aileen Fisher's poem "Skins" describes the textures of the skins of many fruits, featuring textures as varied as those of pineapples and peaches.

Barbara visited with children in a second-grade classroom who responded to these poems with heartfelt discussions of favorite foods and their textures. They decided that they would like to create charts of foods arranged in *textured* categories. In deference to Barbara's favorite, they allowed *smooth foods* to be one of their categories. *Slimy foods* was a favorite category and included the insides of grapes, spaghetti, overcooked spinach, and too-ripe bananas. *Crisp foods* included celery and carrots, potato chips and crackers, apples, and a breakfast cereal that snapped, crackled, and popped. When asked to suggest foods with unique characteristics, one second-grader said she didn't know how to describe how a dried apricot felt on her tongue, but it was like eating something leathery. Another child had tasted okra recently, and like Barbara, found the combination of slimy and hairy textures not to his liking. Barbara suggested that the children match up a food with a texture term that described it, saying she thought the leathery dried apricot and the hairy, slimy okra might be the beginnings of poems. Some children chose to write poems to their favorite foods after this class session, and the notion of textures stayed with them. Later in the school year, when the children visited a local supermarket, they compiled new and improved lists of foods with differing textures and presented them to Barbara by way of their teacher.

Other activities work well in the study of foods. Just as children studying rocks performed a reach-in-the bag texture activity, they might try guessing foods in a bag by feeling for their textures. Another bag activity can be done with primary-grade students who have en-

Goldstein, B. 1998. *The Beastly Feast*. Illus. by Blair Lent. New York: Holt. (P)

Poems about foods are illustrated with appealing pictures.

McMillan, B. 1991. *Eating Fractions*. New York: Scholastic. (P)

Photographs of foods cut into pieces explain fractions at a more sophisticated level.

Pomeroy, D. 1996. *One Potato: A Counting Book of Potato Prints*. San Diego: Harcourt Brace. (P)

Potato prints of vegetables might encourage personal collections of food prints.

Sabuda, R. 1997. *Cookie Count: A Tasty Pop-Up*. New York: Simon & Schuster. (U/P)

Elaborate pop-ups show a variety of special desserts.

Weeks, S. 1997. *Noodles: An Enriched Pop-Up Product*. Illus. by D.A. Carter. New York: HarperCollins. (P)

This pop-up book features the many shapes of pasta.

Stories with Recipes Included

Cordova, A. 1997. *Abuelita's Heart*. New York: Simon & Schuster. (P)

Includes a recipe for a bean dish called "The Happiness Meal."

Darling, B. 1992. *Valerie and the Silver Pear*. Illus. by D. Lane. New York: Four Winds. (P)

Includes a recipe for pear pie.

Devlin, W. & H. Devlin. 1993. *Cranberry Easter*. New York: Simon & Schuster. (P)

Includes a recipe for cranberry cobbler.

_____. 1990. *Cranberry Thanksgiving*. New York: Simon & Schuster. (P)

Includes a recipe for cranberry bread.

De Paola, T. 1978a. *Pancakes for Breakfast*. San Diego: Harcourt Brace. (P)

Includes a recipe for pancakes.

_____. 1978b. *The Popcorn Book*. New York: Holiday. (P)

Includes two ways of making popcorn.

_____. 1985. *Watch Out for Chicken Feet in Your Soup*. New York: Simon & Schuster. (P)

Includes a recipe for chicken soup.

Ehlert, L. 1987. *Growing Vegetable Soup*. San Diego: Harcourt Brace. (P)

Shows processes of vegetable gardening, from seeds to soup, including a recipe.

_____. 1995. *Snowballs*. San Diego: Harcourt Brace. (P)

Includes a recipe for popcorn balls.

Hippely, H.H. 1996. *A Song for Lena*. Illus. by L. Baker. New York: Simon & Schuster. (P)

Includes a recipe for apple strudel.

Polacco, P. 1990. *Thundercake*. New York: Putnam. (P)

Includes a recipe for thundercake.

Rael, E.O. 1996. *What Zeesie Saw on Delancy Street*. Illus. by M. Priceman. New York: Simon & Schuster. (P)

Includes recipes for tsimmes (sweet relish) and leykach (honey cake).

————. 1997. *When Zahdeh Danced on Eldridge Street*. Illus. by M. Priceman. New York: Simon & Schuster. (P)

Includes recipes for apple cake and apricot jam cookies.

Schotter, R. 1998. *Purim Play*. Illus. by M. Hafner. Boston: Little, Brown. (P)

Includes recipe for apricot-orange hamantaschen.

Wing, N. 1995. *Jalapeno Bagels*. Illus. by R. Casilla. New York: Simon & Schuster. (P)

Includes recipes for chango bars and jalapeno bagels.

Cookbooks with Ties to Children's Literature and History

George, J.C. 1995. *Acorn Pancakes, Dandelion Salad, and 38 Other Wild Recipes*. Illus. by P. Mirocha. New York: HarperCollins. (U)

Includes recipes for cooking with plants that are commonly found in the wild.

————. 1982. *The Wild, Wild Cookbook*. Illus. by Walter Kessell. New York: Crowell. (U)

A collection similar to George's *Acorn Pancakes*, this is out of print but available in libraries.

MacDonald, K. 1987. *The Anne of Green Gables Cookbook*. Illus. by B. Dilelle. New York: Oxford. (U)

Recipes for foods that are mentioned in this classic series.

Mayer, M. 1998. *The Mother Goose Cookbook: Rhymes and Recipes for the Very Young*. Illus. by C. Schwartz. New York: Morrow. (P)

Recipes for nursery rhyme food that primary students will love to make.

Penner, L.R. 1991. *Eating the Plates: A Pilgrim Book of Food and Manners*. New York: Simon & Schuster. (P)

A history of the foods, recipes, and menus of early American settlers.

Perl, L. 1979. *Hunter Stew and Hangtown Fry: What Pioneer America Ate and Why*. Illus. by R. Cuffari. Boston: Houghton Mifflin. (U)

————. 1979. *Slumps, Grunts, and Snickerdoodles: What Colonial America Ate and Why*. Illus. by R. Cuffari. Boston: Houghton Mifflin. (U)

Both of these books provide histories of American foodways and ideas for recipes and menus.

Potter, B. 1994. *The Peter Rabbit and Friends Cookbook.* New York: Warner. (P)

This recipe collection includes foods inspired by those loved by Potter's animal characters.

Walker, B. 1979. *The Little House Cookbook.* Illus. by G. Williams. New York: HarperCollins. (U)

Passages from Wilder's books, with simplified recipes for making the dishes that are mentioned.

Texture You Can See

Artists sometimes encourage us to feel texture, even as we look at their illustrations on the flat page. We are invited to use our eyes, our imaginations, and memories of texture to give us a sense of touch in a picture book. Jeannie Baker and Molly Bang's collage art gives us a sense of texture, even though the paper feels flat and two dimensional when we run our hands across it. Faith Ringgold uses the texture of fabrics in her quilted frames for *Tar Beach.* Tana Hoban invites us to think about natural textures and patterns in her books *Just Look, Look Again* and *Take Another Look.* In these books, photographs of natural objects are covered with a frame and a peephole. Readers are invited to make guesses about the subjects in the frames by looking at their textures and patterns. Children may enjoy making their own versions of these visual books, using actual photographs or pictures cut from magazines and creating appropriate frames for the guessing game. Other texture activities might include making textured maps of the classroom or a favorite place, using small scraps of fabric, yarn, foil, and paper of many types. As children create poems and stories, they also can consider what types of texture they might incorporate in their illustrations, just as artists do. They might ask themselves these questions: What textures would help to convey the meaning best? What types of materials could I use to create this texture?

Books That Show Texture

Albert, B. 1993. *Where Does the Trail Lead?* Illus. by B. Pinkney. New York: Simon & Schuster. (P)

Scratchboard illustrations show a young boy following a trail through the countryside to the sea.

Allinson, B. 1990. *Effie*. Illus. by B. Reid. New York: Scholastic. (P)
Plasticine is used to tell the story of an ant with a voice so loud she frightens an elephant away.

Aylesworth, J. 1994. *My Son John*. Illus. by D. Frampton. New York: Holt. (P)
Variations on the traditional nursery rhyme are illustrated with woodcuts in this picture book.

Bunting, E. 1996. *Going Home*. Illus. by D. Diaz. New York: HarperCollins. (P)
Frames for the illustrations for this Christmas story set in Mexico feature collages of traditional Mexican crafts.

Corwin, J.H. 1998. *My First Riddles*. New York: HarperCollins. (P)
Quilted fabric pictures with clues allow readers to predict answers to these simple riddles.

Crews, N. 1997. *Snowball*. New York: Greenwillow. (P)
Cut-out photographs highlight this story about a snowstorm in the city.

Emberly, R. 1998. *My Mother's Secret Life*. Boston: Little, Brown. (P)
Cut paper, feathers, jewels, and other materials are used to create the circus of a girl's mother's secret life.

Field, E. 1998. *Magic Words*. Illus. by S. Vitale. San Diego: Harcourt Brace. (U)
Creation poems inspired by Inuit traditional songs are illustrated with paintings on wood, bark, and stone.

Fonteyn, M. 1998. *Coppelia*. Illus. by S. Johnson & L. Fancher. San Diego: Harcourt Brace. (U/P)
Paintings and fabric combine to give a richness to this retelling of the ballet about a doll that comes to life.

Hale, S.J. 1995. *Mary Had a Little Lamb*. Illus. by S. Mavor. New York: Orchard.
Applique, embroidery, stuffed sculpture pieces, and other techniques enhance this retelling of a classic story.

Hall, D. 1995. *Lucy's Summer*. Illus. by M. McCurdy. San Diego: Harcourt Brace. (P)
Scratchboard illustrations give this and Hall's other Lucy stories an old-fashioned feel.

Hoban, T. 1996. *Just Look*. New York: Greenwillow. (P)
See text.

Hooks, W. 1990. The *Ballad of Belle Dorcas*. Illus. by B. Pinkney. New York: Knopf. (P)
A traditional story about the true love between two slaves who cannot be together except in death is illustrated by scratchboard.

Jackson, E. 1995. *Brown Cow, Green Grass, Yellow Mellow Sun*. Illus. by V. Raymond. New York: Hyperion. (P)

Plastic clay is used to tell this simple story of the processes needed to create the butter for morning pancakes.

MacLachlan, P. 1995. *What You Know First*. Illus. by B. Moser. New York: HarperCollins. (P)

Simple woodcuts give this story of the difficulties of moving away from home in the nineteenth century an historical feel.

Mahy, M. 1987. *17 Kings and 42 Elephants*. Illus. by P. MacCarthy. New York: Dial. (P)

Batik paintings on silk, as well as rhythmic, rhymed text, capture the noise and excitement of a large party making its way through the jungle at night.

Presilla, M. 1996. *Mola: Cuna Life Stories and Art*. New York: Holt. (U/P)

An exploration of the Cuno Indian culture of Panama is illustrated with examples of their embroidered cloth panels, known as molas.

Presilla, M. & G. Soto. 1996. *Life Around the Lake: Embroidery by the Women of Lake Patzcuaro*. New York: Holt. (U/P)

An exploration of the Tarascan culture of Mexico is illustrated with their embroideries.

Shea, P.D. 1995. *The Whispering Cloth: A Refugee's Story*. Illus. by A. Riggio & Y. Yang. Honesdale, PA: Boyds Mills. (P)

Illustrations are taken from a pa'ndau, the embroidery-stitched story cloth of the Hmong.

Soto, G. 1997. *Snapshots from the Wedding*. Illus. by S. Garcia. New York: Putnam. (P)

A young girl tells the high points of a family wedding, and each is revealed through illustrations.

Quilts

Faith Ringgold is perhaps the best-known artist who has used quilts as the basis for her illustrated books for children. *Tar Beach*, which began with a story quilt shown in a photograph in the back of the book, uses quilts as the frames for her story of a joyful family picnic up on the roof of her apartment house on a hot summer night. *Dinner at Aunt Connie's House*, with its gallery of famous African Americans, also uses this design.

Because quilts have existed in many cultures and traditions, many picture books use quilts as a means of communicating pride in one's heritage. Valerie Flournoy's *The Patchwork Quilt* is a picture book story of another African-American family with a tradition of quilt making. Georgia Guback's *Luka's Quilt* is a family story using quilting traditions from Hawaii. Students in many classrooms have worked together to create quilts for display in their schools and communities. The quilts might make use of traditional patterns from early America, or crazy-quilt techniques from African-American tradition, or the lovely flowerwork motifs of Hawaiian quilts.

The patterns and textures of quilts lend themselves to language activities as well. Ann Whitford Paul's *Eight Hands Round: A Patchwork Alphabet* features early American quilt patterns named for each letter of the alphabet. One classroom of third-graders used this book to get ideas for a class quilt, but extended the activity by creating their own alphabet quilts of favorite words, organized in traditional squares and hand-colored on carefully chosen colored backgrounds. These "published" quilts had the quality of concrete poems, each word carefully chosen for its sound and shape on the quilt.

Students who have quilts passed down in their families, as the little girl does in Tony Johnston's *The Quilt Story*, might want to bring these in and share or write their histories for other students in the class. They might want to invite into the classroom quilters from the community who can share information on quilting traditions and how quilts are made. These stories may lead children to try their hands at stories about quilts or other family heirlooms that are passed from one generation to another.

Books on Quilts

Cobb, M. 1995. *The Quilt-Block History of Pioneer Days with Projects Kids Can Make*. Illus. by J.D. Ellis. Brookfield, CT: Millbrook. (U/P)
Designs for quilts created and popularized during the period of the westward movement are used to help convey a history of the time.

Flournoy, V. 1985. *The Patchwork Quilt*. Illus. by J. Pinkney. New York: Dial. (P)
See text.

Geras, A. 1982. *Apricots at Midnight and Other Stories from a Patchwork Quilt*. Illus. by D. Cladwell. New York: Atheneum. (U)
Each patch in an old patchwork quilt reminds Aunt Penny of another story.

Guback, G. 1994. *Luka's Quilt*. New York: Greenwillow. (P)
See text.

Hopkinson, D. 1992. *Sweet Clara and the Freedom Quilt.* Illus. by
J. Ransome. New York: Knopf. (U/P)
Clara uses scraps to create a map of an escape route on the Underground
Railroad, which helps her escape to freedom.

Johnston, T. 1985. *The Quilt Story.* Illus. by T. De Paola. New York: Putnam. (P)
See text.

Kinsey-Warnock, N. 1989. *The Canada Geese Quilt.* Illus. by L.W. Bowman.
New York: Cobblehill. (P)
A special quilt made by her grandmother comforts Ariel during hard times.

Kuskin, K. 1994. *Patchwork Island.* Illus. by P. Mathers. New York:
HarperCollins. (P)
A mother pieces a patchwork quilt that becomes an island of memories
for her child.

Paul, A.W. 1991. *Eight Hands Round: A Patchwork Alphabet.* Illus. by
J. Winter. New York: HarperCollins.
See text.

_____. 1996. *The Seasons Sewn: A Year in Patchwork.* Illus. by M. McCurdy.
San Diego: Harcourt Brace. (U/P)
Quilt patterns are shown and their connections to historical activities in
the nineteenth century are described.

Polacco, P. 1988. *The Keeping Quilt.* New York: Simon & Schuster. (P)
Great Gramma Anna makes a quilt that serves to tie the generations of a
Russian–Jewish family together.

Ringgold, F. 1993. *Aunt Harriet's Underground Railroad in the Sky.* New York:
Crown. (U/P)
Ringgold's story quilt-turned-picture book explores the Underground
Railroad, with Cassie and BeBe discovering the horrors of slavery and
the joy of freedom.

_____. 1993. *Dinner at Aunt Connie's House.* New York: Hyperion. (U/P)
Aunt Connie's paintings come alive and tell their stories in this story
quilt-inspired book.

_____. 1988. *Tar Beach.* New York: Crown. (U/P)
See text.

Collage and Other Paper Constructions

Collage, a term from the French word for "glue," is an assembly of
fragments that are arranged and glued onto a background to create a
unified whole. The elements of collage are easily available in most class-

rooms (pieces of paper, cut pictures, fabric, and strips of words either taken from magazines and newspapers or typed or printed on pieces of paper). Collage, while sophisticated in meaning, has a childlike quality that allows us to be expressive without necessarily having the careful skills required of drawing and painting. Collage activity is often used in conjunction with writing or as a way of collectively experiencing what we have learned about a subject. An individual student may create a collage, or small groups or whole classes of students may work together to turn these fragments into something meaningful.

Like so much of what we have talked about in this book, the collage may look artless, but it is an organized and structured presentation of material. Choices about what pictures, words, colors, and textures to use, and how to arrange them require thought and discussion. Lois Lowry provides a humorous insight into what can go wrong with this process in *Anastasia Krupnik,* when the children, working independently of one another, create a community bulletin board made up of a number of miscellaneous fragments, including pizza stands, several state prisons, and so on. The resulting work is simply a collection of odd items with no unifying theme or understanding of their community. The best collages children create are, like those found in the illustrations of fine picture books, abstract but organized presentations of a topic, theme, or idea.

Collage started to be used in picture books for children in the 1960s and 1970s. During that period, Leo Lionni received four Caldecott Honor Medals for collage illustrations in his books. Ezra Jack Keats won the Caldecott for *The Snowy Day* and received an Honor for *Goggles.* These two illustrators, along with Eric Carle, have been perennially popular with primary-grade children, both for good stories and for the use of this childlike technique. In the past fifteen years, collage and other forms of assembly have emerged in illustrations for students of all ages. An increasing number of books featuring collage and other cut-paper techniques are being published. All provide models for children to consider when they want to express their ideas and stories through textures in art.

A look at the books that convey meaning through collage and other paper constructions reveals that these forms are chosen deliberately because they best convey certain topics and themes. Contemporary books about nature and the environment, from Patricia Mullins' *V for Vanishing* to Jeannie Baker's *The Story of Rosy Dock* to Lois Ehlert's *Red Leaf, Yellow Leaf,* use collage textures to replicate the textures of the natural world they describe. Students also may notice that illustrators may choose collage to illustrate folk tales and mythology, perhaps because these abstract representations in art best capture the magic and metaphor of folklore. Collages might then be students' choice for illustrations of works about nature or magical stories.

![black bar]

Books with Collage or Cut Paper Textures

Baker, J. 1995. *The Story of Rosy Dock*. New York: Greenwillow. (P)
Collage helps tell the story of the planting and spread of this striking Australian plant.

Bang, M. 1985. *The Paper Crane*. New York: Greenwillow. (P)
A folded-paper bird comes alive and saves a restaurant when the owner is kind to a magical stranger.

Bunting, E. 1997. *Ducky*. Illus. by D. Wisniewski. New York: Clarion. (P)
Cut-paper illustrations help tell of the journey of one of the twenty-nine thousand plastic ducks that were washed overboard from a ship in a 1992 storm.

———. 1995. *Smoky Night*. Illus. by D. Diaz. San Diego: Harcourt Brace. (P)
Elaborate collage frames featuring found objects from city sidewalks illustrate this story set during the Los Angeles riots.

Carle, E. 1990. *The Very Quiet Cricket*. New York: Philomel. (P)
See text.

Cassedy, S. & K. Suetake. 1992. *Red Dragonfly on My Shoulder*. Illus. by M. Bang. New York: HarperCollins. (P)
Collages from found objects help make the imagery in these haiku poems explicit.

Cendrars, B. 1982. *Shadow*. Illus. by M. Brown. New York: Simon & Schuster. (P)
Cut out painted shapes and wood cuts printed in white ink capture the landscape and spirits in this story set in Africa.

Collard, S.B. 1997. *Animal Dads*. Illus. by S. Jenkins. Boston: Houghton Mifflin. (P)
Simple textured-paper collages represent various male animals who care for their young.

Ehlert, L. 1991. *Red Leaf, Yellow Leaf*. San Diego: Harcourt Brace. (P)
See text.

———. 1995. *Snowballs*. San Diego: Harcourt Brace. (P)
Cut paper and objects such as mittens, seeds, and popcorn are arranged in this book about aspects of snow.

Emberly, R. 1995. *Three Cool Kids*. Boston: Little, Brown. (P)

Cut paper collage is used in this modern retelling of *The Three Billy Goats Gruff*.

Fleming, D. 1998. *Mama Cat Has Three Kittens*. New York: Holt. (P)

Fleming uses paints and handmade paper for collage in this and her other books about animals.

Frasier, D. 1991. *On the Day You Were Born*. San Diego: Harcourt Brace. (P)

Collages show all of the natural events taking place on earth on the day a child was born.

Hughes, L. 1995. *The Block*. Illus. by R. Beardon. New York: Viking. (U)

Twelve poems are used to highlight aspects of Romare Bearden's 1971 collage of Harlem.

Jenkins, S. 1997. *What Do You Do When Something Wants to Eat You?* Boston: Houghton Mifflin. (P)

Collages illustrate animal camouflage and defense mechanisms.

Keats, E.J. 1969. *Goggles*. New York: Macmillan. (P)

———. 1963. *The Snowy Day*. New York: Viking. (P)

See text.

Lenski, L. 1996. *Sing a Song of People*. Illus. by G. Larouche. Boston: Little, Brown. (P)

The joys of city life are explored in this cut paper–illustrated rhyme.

Lionni, L. 1964. *Swimmy*. New York: Knopf. (P)

———. 1967. *Frederick*. New York: Knopf. (P)

———. 1969. *Alexander and the Wind-Up Mouse*. New York: Pantheon. (P)

———. 1994. *An Extraordinary Egg*. New York: Knopf. (P)

———. 1995. *Inch by Inch*. New York: Morrow. (P)

One of the earliest illustrators to use collage, Lionni has used this medium in increasingly sophisticated ways.

MacDonald, S. & B. Oakes. 1990. *Once upon Another: The Tortoise and the Hare and the Lion and the Mouse*. New York: Doubleday. (P)

Two stories are interwoven in this sophisticated use of collage.

Marzollo, J. 1998. *I Am a Rock*. Illus. by J. Moffatt. New York: Scholastic. (U/P)

Collage highlights this collection of riddles about rocks and minerals.

Mullins, P. 1994. *V for Vanishing: An Alphabet of Endangered Animals*. New York: HarperCollins. (P)

See text.

Stafford, K. 1994. *We Got Here Together*. Illus. by D. Frasier. San Diego: Harcourt Brace. (U/P)

Tie-died papers are cut to create the shape and feel of water in this book featuring the water cycle.

With spaces left for adding information, checklists, pictures, and drawings, these simple books give students models for items to include in their own scrapbooks.

Belton, S. 1996. *Ernestine and Amanda*. New York: Simon & Schuster. (U)

————. 1997. *Ernestine and Amanda: Summer Camp, Ready or Not!* New York: Simon & Schuster. (U)

A scrapbook of photographs and historical context is provided in the back of each of these brief novels about a friendship between two very different girls who start out as enemies.

Blocksma, M. 1993. *Ticket to the Twenties*. Illus. by S. Dennen. Boston: Little, Brown. (U/P)

See text.

Cole, J. & B. Degen. *The Magic School Bus* Series. New York: Scholastic. (P)

See text.

Fleischman, P. 1996. *Dateline: Troy*. Cambridge, MA: Candlewick. (U)

Contemporary newspaper clippings are paired with ancient Greek legends to give new life to these old stories.

Frasier, D. 1998. *Out of the Ocean*. San Diego: Harcourt Brace. (P)

Cut paper and beach artifacts illustrate photographs in this poetic description of life on the seashore.

Joyce, W. 1997. *The World of William Joyce Scrapbook*. New York: HarperCollins. (U)

Drawings, photographs, and hand-printed text show Joyce's life and inspiration for his strange works of fantasy.

Krupinski, L. 1997. *Into the Woods: A Woodland Scrapbook*. New York: HarperCollins. (U/P)

Hand-written text and many pictures model nature scrapbooks.

————. 1994. *A New England Scrapbook: A Journey Through Poetry, Prose, and Pictures*. New York: HarperCollins. (U/P)

See text.

Levinson, N. 1985. *Watch the Stars Come Out*. Illus. by D. Goode. New York: Dutton. (P)

See text.

Masoff, J. 1998. *Fire!* Illus. by J. Riznicki & B.D. Smith. New York: Scholastic. (U/P)

This scrapbook shows fire-fighting techniques, materials, types of fires, and pictures of people who fight fires.

Moss, M. 1997. *Amelia Hits the Road*. Berkeley, CA: Tricycle Press. (U/P)

Amelia's journal includes pictures and comments that students might want to include in a personal journal.

Spedden, D.C.S. 1994. *Polar the Titanic Bear*. Illus. by L. McGraw. Boston: Little, Brown. (P)

Photographs, drawings, and historical information, along with diary entries, tell the story of a stuffed bear that traveled on and survived the sinking of the Titanic.

Willard, N. & J. Dyer. 1997. *Cracked Corn and Snow Ice Cream*. San Diego: Harcourt Brace. (U)

See text.

■■■■■■■■■■

It is from the artifacts of understanding we collect in scrapbooks that we begin to piece together the story of our lives. Photographs, clippings, quotations, poems, lists, and small objects can be the pieces we use to weave together the pattern of who we are, for ourselves and for others, through writing, art, and storytelling. Each encounter we have with ways of ordering the world around us, through the lens of the scientist, the mathematician, the artist, or the poet, opens our eyes to another way of seeing. These collections of thoughts, ideas, and experiences, when explored and reflected on in classrooms where the edges are blurred, give us lessons in how to understand and live successfully in the world.

Conclusion

As we put this book together, we tried to think about a variety of ways to model an integrated elementary school curriculum—one in which the elements of writing process and good books help children to think about and understand individual disciplines and the ways these disciplines interact and connect. We shared a variety of types of writing. We looked at author studies and suggested ideas for using a variety of books across the curriculum. We included units on archaeology, geology, the sense of touch, animal behavior, and the study of the stars. We probed attitudes toward mathematics, and worked on counting and large numbers. We included artistic puzzles and riddles, collage and paper construction, texture, and creation of scrapbooks. We explored ancient mysteries, historic events, and holidays. We tried to show links across the curriculum through several units.

But the works we have explored here are just the beginning of the connections we might make across the curriculum. One of our favorite books/poems is Mary Ann Hoberman's *A House Is a House for Me*, in which she explores all the things that could be thought of, metaphorically, as houses, including books as houses for stories, and pens as homes for ink (Hoberman 1978). At the end of her long rollicking lists of houses, she begins to worry that she is "far-fetching," seeing everything though her glorious metaphor of the house. This is both the delight and the caution for making links across the curriculum. As we work with our students, our curriculum, and good books, possibilities emerge at every turn. We need to consider which links are natural, giving rise to questions that reveal differences in how people in different disciplines might view the world. We need to invite students to try new ways of thinking about the world and to keep ourselves from far-fetching simply because we notice overlapping terms or concepts. The critical thinking and follow-up behind links across disciplines is the most significant part of interdisciplinary study.

To this end, we include some questions that we ask whenever we embark on interdisciplinary study:

- How can we incorporate more meaningful reading activities into this activity?
- How can we encourage children to write for authentic purposes about what they are learning?
- How can we encourage children to look at this subject from more than one perspective or point of view?
- Are we allowing children to make connections among books they read and ideas they express, rather than trying to force linkages in order to cover more material?
- Are we creating an environment in our classrooms that encourages these connections, an environment that is
  - flexible, so that children have time to explore ideas without interruptions?
  - rich in literature, with lots of folklore, fiction, well-written nonfiction, and poetry available for children to read?
  - rich in language, with models for poetry, prose writing, drafting, revising, and beautiful finished work available for children to experience?
  - rich in opportunities for discovery, with centers filled with objects and activities children can see, touch, taste, smell, hear, manipulate, try out, and explore, which might provide the questions and models from which they can build an interdisciplinary curriculum with our help?

There are a number of ways to begin to develop these linkages. We suggest starting small, trying to find links between two subjects or genres of literature or forms of writing, rather than including everything you might see as a link. A unit on change, for example, is nearly overwhelming for children, as well as their teacher, because the topic is so large. Instead, consider some miniunits on change, which over the course of a year allow this theme to be explored in a number of ways. Change can be studied at any grade, because it is integral to all study. It might be approached through science, with units on seasons, metamorphosis, and human growth and development, using the science notebooks and scrapbooks discussed in Chapters Five and Six, respectively. It might be entered through the social studies, as children ponder changes in themselves, their friendships, their communities, and the history of the nation and the world through study of literature;

through diaries, journals, and letters; and through historical study. For primary students, it might begin with a study of transformations in traditional literature and fantasy, wherein characters are transformed from frogs into princes and mice into coachmen. For older readers, it might begin with a novel such as Natalie Babbitt's *Tuck Everlasting*, in which time stands still and nothing changes for the Tuck family, with terrible consequences. It might begin with the writing process, as we did in this volume. Revision is natural not only to student writers, but also to the authors they love to read.

There are always a number of points at which we can enter a study. No one of these is the right way to begin. Our students' interests, the time available, and links across the curriculum may provide entrance points, and these can change each time we approach a topic or theme. The following are a number of possible starting points, each with ideas for the different directions in which these may take us:

- We might share a favorite picture book and consider responses and questions raised by its themes or topics. Barbara loves Barbara Cooney's *Miss Rumphius* (1982) because, like the main character, Barbara has been a librarian, has lived in a house by the sea, and loves the colors and smells of lupines. The book's message, that we should each do something to make the world more beautiful, lends itself to writing and drawing, through which students can create their own versions of this more beautiful place. Or, we might choose to look at Barbara Cooney's illustrated books and study her style of illustration, or study wildflowers and the processes by which they reseed and spread, or even consider how different it might be to live by the sea, in the mountains, or on the open prairie.

- A favorite novel might be an invitation to blur the edges. When students read Karen Hesse's *Out of the Dust* (1997), they may be surprised to see that this novel takes the form of a series of poems, and a conversation about genres and forms might follow. Students may want to try their hands at writing their own poems that reveal something about a character or incident the way the novel does. *Out of the Dust*, which describes the life of an Oklahoma family during the Depression, may pique interest in further reading and study about this period, inviting readings from such classic novels as Doris Gates' *Blue Willow* (1940) or Mildred Taylor's *Roll of Thunder Hear My Cry* (1976). It might spark interest in the causes of the Dust Bowl and the impor-

There is no right way to create a collage curriculum in which lines are blurred. By pooling our imaginations and experiences with those of our students, we enrich the curriculum, creating linkages that capitalize on student concerns and wonders. Opportunities for reading, writing, and talking expand our understandings and raise new questions to explore. When we embrace a multigenre, interdisciplinary curriculum as a means for instruction, we find reading and writing in ordinary places. Poet Georgia Heard is right—language is lurking in our classrooms when we change our way of looking for it (Heard 1995, 6).

References

Atwell, N. 1990. *Coming to Know.* Portsmouth, NH: Heinemann.

Avi. 1990. *The True Confessions of Charlotte Doyle.* New York: Orchard.

———. 1991. *Nothing but the Truth: A Documentary Novel.* New York: Orchard.

Babbitt, N. 1975. *Tuck Everlasting.* New York: Farrar, Straus.

Baylor, B. 1986. *I'm in Charge of Celebrations.* Illus. by P. Parnall. New York: Scribners.

———. 1993. *Desert Voices.* Illus. by P. Parnall. New York: Scribners.

Bergen, D., ed. 1987. *Play as a Medium for Learning and Development.* Portsmouth, NH: Heinemann.

Berry, J. 1996. *Rough Sketch: Beginning.* Illus. by R. Florczak. San Diego: Harcourt Brace.

Breathed, B. 1994. *Red Ranger Came Calling.* Boston: Little, Brown.

Buchanan, K. & D. Buchanan. 1994. *It Rained in the Desert Today.* Illus. by L. Tracy. Flagstaff, AZ: Northland.

———. 1991. *The Moon and I.* Englewood Cliffs, NJ: Julian Messner.

Chatton, B. & N.D. Collins. 1995. "Always Wondering." *Writing Teacher* 8 (5): 18–22. (ECS Learning Systems, Inc. PO Box 791437, San Antonio, TX 78279)

Cleary, B. 1950. *Henry Huggins.* New York: Morrow.

———. 1981. *Ramona Quimby, Age Eight.* New York: Morrow.

———. 1983. *Dear Mr. Henshaw.* New York: Morrow.

———. 1988. *A Girl From Yamhill.* New York: Morrow.

———. 1990. *Muggie Maggie.* New York: Morrow.

Collier, J. & C. Collier. 1984. *My Brother Sam Is Dead.* New York: Simon & Schuster.

Conrad, P. 1989. *The Tub People.* New York: HarperCollins.

Cooney, B. 1982. *Miss Rumphius.* New York: Viking.

Corbishley, M. 1990. *Detecting the Past.* New York: Gloucester Press.

Esbensen, B.J. 1990. *Great Northern Diver: The Loon.* Boston: Little, Brown.

_____. 1992. *Who Shrank My Grandmother's House? Poems of Discovery.* Illus. by E. Beddowes. New York: HarperCollins.

Fisher, A. 1966. *Valley of the Smallest: The Life Story of the Shrew.* New York: Crowell.

Fleischman, S. 1986. *The Whipping Boy.* New York: Greenwillow.

_____. 1996. *The Abracadabra Kid: A Writer's Life.* New York: Greenwillow.

Forbes, E. 1943. *Johnny Tremain.* Boston: Houghton Mifflin.

Fuller, T. 1983. "Writing Is Everybody's Business." *Phi Kappa Phi* 65 (4): 21–24.

Gates, D. 1940. *Blue Willow.* Illus. by P. Lantz. New York: Viking.

Graves, D. 1994. *A Fresh Look at Writing.* Portsmouth, NH: Heinemann.

Greene, R.G. 1997. *When a Line Bends . . . A Shape Begins.* Illus. by J. Kaczman. Boston: Houghton Mifflin.

Hanff, H. 1975. *84 Charing Cross Road.* New York: Viking.

Heard, G. 1995. *Writing Toward Home.* Portsmouth, NH: Heinemann.

Hesse, K. 1997. *Out of the Dust.* New York: Scholastic.

Hoban, T. 1986. *Shapes, Shapes, Shapes.* New York: Greenwillow.

Hoberman, M. 1978. *A House Is a House for Me.* New York: Viking.

Kovacs, D. & J. Preller. 1991. *Meet the Authors and Illustrators.* New York: Scholastic.

Kuskin, K. 1980. "Thistles." In *Dogs and Dragons, Trees and Dreams.* New York: HarperCollins.

Leedy, L. 1997. *Measuring Penny.* New York: Holt.

Locker, T. 1995. *Sky Tree: Seeing Science Through Art.* New York: HarperCollins.

Lowry, L. 1979. *Anastasia Krupnik.* Boston: Houghton Mifflin.

Macaulay, D. 1980. *Unbuilding.* Boston: Houghton Mifflin.

McClure, A. & J.V. Kristo, eds. 1996. *Books That Invite Talk, Wonder, and Play.* Urbana, IL: National Council of Teachers of English.

Merriam, E. 1986. *A Sky Full of Poems.* New York: Dell.

Moffett, J. & B.J. Wagner. 1992. *Student-Centered Language Arts, K–12.* 4th ed. Portsmouth, NH: Boynton/Cook.

Mullins, P. 1994. *V for Vanishing.* New York: HarperCollins.

Murray, D.M. 1996. *Writing to Learn.* New York: Holt.

Nichol, B. 1993. *Beethoven Lives Upstairs.* Illus. by S. Cameron. New York: Orchard.

O'Laughlin, M. 1997. Writing Lives: The Writing Processes of Children's Authors and Their Characters. Doctoral Dissertation, University of Wyoming, 1997. Dissertation Abstracts International, AAG9805272.

Paterson, K. 1988. *The Author's Eye.* New York: Random House Media.

Peet, B. 1989. *Bill Peet: An Autobiography*. Boston: Houghton Mifflin.

Probst, R. 1988. *Response and Analysis: Teaching Literature in Junior and Senior High School*. Portsmouth, NH: Boynton/Cook.

Quinn, T. 1997. *Transactional Paper*. Gillette, WY: Wyoming Writing Project.

Richards, L. 1990. "Measuring Things in Words: Language for Learning Mathematics." *Language Arts* 7 (1): 14–25.

Romano, T. 1987. *Clearing the Way*. Portsmouth, NH: Heinemann.

———. 1995. *Writing with Passion*. Portsmouth, NH: Heinemann.

Rylant, C. 1988. *All I See*. New York: Orchard.

———. 1992. *Missing May*. New York: Dutton.

———. 1993. *The Relatives Came*. New York: Simon & Schuster.

Sendak, M. 1963. *Where the Wild Things Are*. New York: HarperCollins.

Seuss, Dr. 1966. *The Cat in the Hat*. New York: Random House.

Smith, F. 1986. *Insult to Intelligence: The Bureaucratic Invasion of Our Classrooms*. Portsmouth, NH: Heinemann.

———. 1992. "Learning to Read: The Never-Ending Debate." *Phi Delta Kappan* 74 (2): 432–41.

Snyder, Z.K. 1991. *Libby on Wednesday*. New York: Dell.

Stanley, D. 1996. *Leonardo da Vinci*. New York: Morrow.

Stevens, C. 1993. *A Book of Your Own: Keeping a Diary or Journal*. New York: Clarion.

Taylor, M. 1976. *Roll of Thunder Hear My Cry*. Illus. by Jerry Pinkney. New York: Dial.

Tchudi, S. & S. Lafer. 1996. *The Interdisciplinary Teacher's Handbook: Integrated Teaching Across the Curriculum*. Portsmouth, NH: Boynton/Cook.

Van Allsburg, C. 1981. *Jumanji*. Boston: Houghton Mifflin.

———. 1982. *Ben's Dream*. Boston: Houghton Mifflin.

———. 1984. *The Mysteries of Harris Burdick*. Boston: Houghton Mifflin.

Viorst, J. 1971. *Alexander and the Terrible, Horrible, No Good, Very Bad Day*. New York: Simon & Schuster.

Weil, L. 1991. *Wolferl: The First Six Years in the Life of Wolfgang Amadeus Mozart*. New York: Holiday.

Weil, Z. 1992. "The Paper Bag." In *Mud, Moon, and Me*. Boston: Houghton Mifflin.

White, E.B. 1952. *Charlotte's Web*. New York: HarperCollins.

Wilkerson, V. 1997. *Transactional Paper*. Gillette, WY: Wyoming Writing Project.

Yolen, J. 1979. *The Giants Go Camping*. New York: Clarion.

For Further Reading

General Works

Bosma, B. & N.D. Guth. 1995. *Children's Literature in an Integrated Curriculum: The Authentic Voice*. Newark, DE: International Reading Association.

Collins, N.D. & B. Chatton. 1993. "Integrating Reading and Writing Instruction: Blurring the Edges." *Writing Teacher* 6 (3): 28–33.

Hickman, J. & B. Cullinan, eds. 1994. *Children's Literature in the Classroom: Extending Charlotte's Web*. Needham Heights, MA: Christopher Gordon.

Hickman, J. & S. Hepler, eds. 1989. *Children's Literature in the Classroom: Weaving Charlotte's Web*. Needham Heights, MA: Christopher Gordon.

McClure, A. & J.V. Kristo eds. 1996. *Books That Invite Talk, Wonder, and Play*. Urbana, IL: National Council of Teachers of English.

Pappas, C.C., B.Z. Kiefer & L.S. Levstik. 1990. *An Integrated Language Perspective in the Elementary School: Theory into Action*. White Plains, NY: Longman.

Pigdon, K. & M. Woolley, eds. 1993. *The Big Picture: Integrating Children's Learning*. Portsmouth, NH: Heinemann.

Walmsley, S.A. 1994. *Children Exploring Their World: Theme Teaching in the Elementary School*. Portsmouth, NH: Heinemann.

The Writing Process/Author Studies

Atwell, N. 1987. *In the Middle: Writing, Reading, and Learning with Adolescents*. Portsmouth, NH: Heinemann.

———. 1990. *Coming to Know: Writing to Learn in the Intermediate Grades*. Portsmouth, NH: Heinemann.

Britton, J. 1993. *Language and Learning*. 2d ed. London: Allen Lane.

Calkins, L. 1983. *Lessons from a Child*. Portsmouth, NH: Heinemann.

Christie, J., B. Enx & C. Vukelich. 1997. *Teaching Language and Literacy: Preschool Through Elementary Grades*. White Plains, NY: Longman.

Clay, M. 1975. *What Did I Write: Beginning Writing Behavior*. Portsmouth, NH: Heinemann.

Downing, C. 1997. "After School Authors." *Book Links* 6 (4): 20–33.

Fisher, B. 1991. *Joyful Learning*. Portsmouth, NH: Heinemann.

Graves, D. 1983. *Writing: Teachers and Children at Work*. Portsmouth, NH: Heinemann.

———. 1994. *A Fresh Look at Writing*. Portsmouth, NH: Heinemann.

Harwayne, S. 1992. *Lasting Impressions*. Portsmouth, NH: Heinemann.

Hepler, S. 1997. "The Writing Life: Autobiographical Reflections." *Book Links* 6 (4): 4–48.

Hepler, S. & D. Bradley. 1997. "The Writing Life, Part II: Struggling with Words." *Book Links* 7 (2): 25–42.

Moffett, J. & B.J. Wagner. 1992. *Student-Centered Language Arts, K–12.* 4th ed. Portsmouth, NH: Boynton/Cook.

Murray, D.M. 1989. *Expecting the Unexpected: Teaching Myself—and Others—to Read and Write.* Portsmouth, NH: Heinemann.

Rief, L. 1992. *Seeking Diversity: Language Arts with Adolescents.* Portsmouth, NH: Heinemann.

Romano, T. 1987. *Clearing the Way: Working with Teenage Writers.* Portsmouth, NH: Heinemann.

————. 1995. *Writing with Passion.* Portsmouth, NH: Heinemann.

Routman, R. 1996. *Literacy at the Crossroads.* Portsmouth, NH: Heinemann.

Mystery/Magic/History/Historical Fiction/Picture Books

Bauer, C.F. 1996. "Magic in the Classroom." *Book Links* 2 (4): 60–63.

Flack, J.D. 1990. *Mystery and Detection: Thinking and Problem Solving with the Sleuths.* Englewood, CO: Libraries Unlimited.

Freeman, E.B. & D.G. Person, eds. 1992. *Using Nonfiction Trade Books in the Elementary Classroom: From Ants to Zeppelins.* Urbana, IL: National Council of Teachers of English.

Gerson, L. 1993. "Journey to Topaz by Yoshiko Uchida." *Book Links* 2 (4): 59–64.

Hickman, J. & B. Cullinan, eds. 1989. *Children's Literature in the Classroom: Weaving Charlotte's Web.* Needham Heights, MA: Christopher Gordon.

Kiefer, B.Z. 1995. *The Potential of Picturebooks: From Visual Literacy to Aesthetic Understanding.* Englewood Cliffs, NJ: Prentice Hall.

Levstik, L.S. & K.C. Barton. 1997. *Doing History: Investigating with Children in Elementary and Middle Schools.* Mahwah, NJ: Lawrence Erlbaum.

McClure, A. & J.V. Kristo, eds. 1996. *Books That Invite Talk, Wonder, and Play.* Urbana, IL: National Council of Teachers of English.

Scales, P. 1994. "Ajeemah and His Son by James Berry." *Book Links* 3 (3): 15–18.

Tunnell, M.O. & R. Ammon. 1995. *The Story of Ourselves: Teaching History Through Children's Literature.* Portsmouth, NH: Heinemann.

Journals/Diaries/Letters

Gantos, J. 1998. "The Next Level: Using Journals to Write Great Short Stories." *Book Links* 7 (5): 19–23.

Girard, S. 1996. *Partnerships for Classroom Learning: From Reading Buddies to the Community and the World Beyond.* Portsmouth, NH: Heinemann.

Paterra, E. 1997. "Letters in Biographies and Novels." *Book Links* 6 (5): 37–39.

Index